MY DECLARATION
——— OF ———
INDEPENDENCE

SENATOR JAMES M. JEFFORDS

INDEPENDENT-VERMONT

SIMON & SCHUSTER

NEW YORK LONDON TORONTO SYDNEY SINGAPORE

SIMON & SCHUSTER
Rockefeller Center
1230 Avenue of the Americas
New York, NY 10020

SIMON & SCHUSTER and colophon are registered trademarks
of Simon & Schuster, Inc.

For information about special discounts for bulk purchases,
please contact Simon & Schuster Special Sales:
1-800-456-6798 or business@simonandschuster.com

Designed by Jeanette Olender
Manufactured in the United States of America

1   3   5   7   9   10   8   6   4   2

Library of Congress Cataloging-in-Publication Data is available

ISBN 0-7432-2842-1

To all Vermonters, by birth or by choice, and especially

to Liz, Laura, Leonard, Maura, and my sister Mary

CONTENTS

MY DECLARATION OF
INDEPENDENCE

WHEN in the Course of human events, it be-
comes necessary for one people to dissolve the
political bands which have connected them with
another, and to assume among the powers of the
earth, the separate and equal station to which
the Laws of Nature and of Nature's God entitle
them, a decent respect to the opinions of man-
kind requires that they should declare the causes
which impel them to the separation.

DECLARATION OF INDEPENDENCE
JULY 4, 1776

ONE

Obscure Senator, Small State

I MUST have walked the corridors of National Airport, now named Reagan National, seven or eight hundred times heading home to Vermont. Though people may imagine the life of a Senator as somewhat distant and glorious, for much of our lives we are first cousins of the traveling salesman. Marriages fail, children suffer, and friends are lost. If this time my mood was on the gloomy side, it was because I had just left a meeting where I had very likely lost a few more friends. It was easily the toughest meeting of the thousands I have had during my three decades in politics.

I was heading for Burlington, Vermont, the trip I had made so many times before, but tonight's eight o'clock flight was anything but routine. Although I had yet to fully appreciate this fact, the people at the airline had, and I had been steered by the airline's personnel to a VIP lounge just beyond the security checkpoint.

It seemed like the first half hour in days that I had a chance to catch my breath. The morning papers scattered about the room had given the story of my considering leaving front-page coverage with photos. The television was running the story almost constantly. Even the business news gave it play, attributing some of the movement in the stock market to speculation about my pending announcement.

My press secretary, Erik Smulson, had been so deluged by phone calls from reporters and producers that this was his first chance to see what was going on around us. Like me, he was amazed by the wall-to-wall coverage. Erik's job had been transformed over the past few days from trying to generate news to trying to contain it at some manageable level.

As the flight's departure time neared, we left the lounge and headed down the corridor to Gate 35A, the low-tech launching pad for the jets and prop planes headed for the small cities of the East Coast. I soon realized why the airline staff had intervened. A hundred yards away, dozens of reporters had staked out the little gate, with TV cameras and microphones pointed my way. This was not going to be another milk run to Burlington.

Before I reached the press, I got my first taste that my deliberations had pierced the veil of public indifference that often attends what Congress does or does not do.

On both sides of the broad aisle, passengers awaiting their flight stood on their chairs and started cheering and applauding, while others pushed forward to shake my hand. This for someone who a few days before may have ranked about 99th on the U.S. Senate celebrity scale.

People don't much care what Congress does, and in a democracy, that can be a very good thing. There are, and should be, more important things in people's lives than who a Senator from a small state might be, or what he might do. But here were scores of people who not only recognized me but also approved of what they thought I would be doing the next day in Vermont, who literally wanted to reach out and touch me. It was extraordinary that the glare of media attention in just a few days had thrust me before people's eyes in a way that was flattering but not entirely comfortable. How had what I thought or done to that point so touched these people?

After running the press gauntlet, something I had some practice in after the past few days, my wife Liz, Erik, my chief of staff, Susan Russ, and I rode a shuttle bus out across the tarmac to the plane.

I had tried throughout the past few days to keep a level head about me, but my family and staff took no chances. Lest I had invested too much meaning into the reception I had just received, Susan pointed out that the people cheering me were waiting for a plane to Boston, hardly a political cross section of the country.

Our plane was a small jet, three seats across, which was a blessing for the Vermont delegation in Congress compared to the small props connecting through Pittsburgh or LaGuardia that used to be our only alternative. The flight usually had a Vermont flavor—a few students from the University, an engineer from IBM, a state employee or two heading home from a conference in Washington, sometimes even Ben or Jerry. It is pretty common to know a few people on the trip; such is the size of my state.

But tonight the press had commandeered it. Within a few minutes of announcing at midday that I would travel to Vermont to make a statement the next day, the seats were sold out (which is not saying all that much, I suppose). UVM may have been represented on the flight, but so were the network news shows, newspapers from London, Dallas, Los Angeles, and Tokyo, and camera crews from who knows where.

But it was not all strangers. The father of my former state director was on the flight, though I have to admit it was awkward seeing him. His daughter had left my office and with my support had won a job in the new Bush Administration, as head of the Vermont–New Hampshire

USDA Rural Development office. Hers is one of a handful of jobs in a state that a Senator can have a role in filling when the President is from the same party. She is immensely qualified and a good Republican, but who could know her fate at that point? Would my candidates for the Vermont U.S. Attorney, U.S. Marshal, and Farm Service Agency Director jobs be at risk as well? Yet more people whose lives my decision would touch.

My wife Liz, one of the people most affected, was seated next to me on the plane. While normally as voluble as I am quiet, she had little to say as we settled in for the flight. Over the past week, we had said about all there was to say on the topic of my party affiliation.

Liz is an independent soul, but she has to be labeled a liberal. How else do you describe someone who was an early supporter of Reverend Jesse Jackson's bid for the presidency, and who put up a yard sign for the Democrat running for Governor the same year I was running as a Republican for the U.S. Senate?

In the instant and sometimes inaccurate analysis that characterized much of the coverage of my decision, Liz was rumored by some to have been the catalyst for my switch, when in fact the opposite was true. She thought it was a bad idea, said so repeatedly and in very unvarnished terms, but gave me tremendous support once she realized my decision was close to being made. She is not one to stand meekly by her man. But I think she realized the anguish I was enduring and wanted me to do what I thought was right.

It may be hard to understand if you are fed a steady diet of caricatures, but the Senate consists of real people, many of whom have personalities as magnetic as their political views can be repellent. I thought Liz would be the last to place much stock in the relationships you can develop in Washington. I traveled home to Vermont almost every weekend. She chose to spend most of her time there, leaving our home on the back side of Killington Mountain only once or twice a year to visit Washington, D.C. But she found, as I did, that political views do not always provide a window on someone's personality. Senator Jesse Helms and his wife, Dorothy, would not agree with Liz on many issues, but they are two of the nicest people you could ever meet.

Is it possible to divorce political views from your opinion of a person? I think so, and I could not function in the Senate otherwise. How corrosive it would be to constantly recalibrate your approach to an individual based on whether you agreed or disagreed on the last vote.

A conservative Republican lobbyist who once spent much of a weekend with Liz and me remarked of her afterward that he had never so thoroughly enjoyed a person with whom he so completely disagreed. My response was "Me, too." It got a good laugh, but in fact Liz and my views are not that far apart, and on the issue of my switch we had made our peace. I had explained to Liz again and again why I was thinking of casting off my Republican label. But she couldn't shake the hurt it would cause our friends, whom she was fond of despite being political opposites.

She also questioned why I would make such a decision so late in my career and whether it would overshadow all else. Neither of us could know how the public, and particularly Vermonters, would receive it. Would I be seen in a harsh light, as petulant or prideful, or could people come to understand my reasoning? What kind of repercussions would flow from it? And as Liz knew better than anyone else, rocky relations with the Republican Party were nothing new; indeed, they have characterized my entire political career in Vermont and Washington, D.C. We had coped with it for thirty years. Why now?

The explanations I had given her were much the same as those I had provided in my meeting a few hours earlier in the Capitol.

At the behest of John Warner, the senior Senator from Virginia and the picture of a southern gentleman, I had joined a small group of Senators in the Vice President's Room, a small, ornate ceremonial office off the floor of the Senate chamber, just before leaving for the airport. John is a tremendously decent and honorable man, and it is almost impossible to say no to him. The room is controlled by the President of the Senate—the role assigned by the Constitution to the Vice President of the United States, Dick Cheney. It had become familiar surroundings over the past few weeks.

Though I agreed to join my colleagues, I knew it would be miserable. How do you explain abandoning your allegiance to the Republican Party to a group of people that will be hurt both personally and professionally?

One of the people in the room, Senator Chuck Grassley of Iowa, came to the Congress with me in January of 1975. The two of us washed up into the House of Representatives in the midst of the Democratic tidal wave caused by Watergate. Voters elected 75 Democrats that fall, and only 17 Republicans. Thanks to my two terms as an active Attorney General in Vermont, I had eked out a narrow 53 percent victory.

Chuck was hobbling around on crutches from a sports injury, and I wore a neck brace from being rear-ended in my car in the last weeks of the campaign. As we walked down the center aisle of the House, probably still more than a little amazed at our surroundings, one Democratic wag remarked, "There's two we almost got."

Chuck and I served on the House Agriculture Committee for years, and he preceded me to the U.S. Senate in 1981. He had slowly worked his way up the seniority ladder so that finally, in January 2001, he became the chairman of a major committee, the powerful Senate Committee on Finance, for the first time in his congressional career.

As we sat in the Vice President's Room, the question Chuck and everyone asked was "How could you do this to us?" They would lose the power some of them had acquired only a few months prior. And while the power of a chairmanship in an evenly divided Senate is far from absolute, it is still considerable. With it, they had hoped to advance the causes and dreams that were as important to them as mine to me.

By the end of the meeting I had tears in my eyes, as did many of the Senators sitting around me. It was gutwrenching trying to explain what impelled me to think of leaving the party, handing control of the Senate to the Democrats and wresting it from my friends and colleagues. By the time I left the meeting, I had agreed to rethink whether I really could decide the course of the

Senate by myself. It was the first time in the past ten days that I had genuine second thoughts.

I sat on the plane, inches from Liz, but entirely alone. How could I arrogate to myself this power, when I had been elected by fewer than 200,000 people in Vermont? How could I exact such a price from my friends? I turned these questions over again and again in my head as we made the 90-minute flight to Vermont. There were no easy answers.

But I knew that if I went ahead, I would have to deliver the speech of my life the next morning. So I worked on the speech draft, reading and rereading the text, adding a few words here, marking for a break there.

My critics are right about one thing. I am not God's gift to oratory. I envy those of my colleagues who could talk a dog off a meat wagon. But that's not me. The *Vermont Owner's Manual,* by Frank Bryan and Bill Mares is a small humor book on Vermont that tries to explain the state to natives and newcomers alike. In its section on which laws are to be taken seriously and which are not, it describes a twenty-minute high school graduation speech by our governor as a misdemeanor, and the same by me as a felony.

Fortunately Vermont is a small enough place that people can know you for your deeds as well as your words.

You can still engage in retail politics, walking down Main Street, working the crowds at the county fairs, and greeting people outside the plant gate. At one point a question on a political survey showed that a third of the voters had met me or attended a meeting I had spoken at. (I'm hoping they are not the third that consistently voted against me.) It is also a state that is fiercely independent. While there is no party registration, polls show about half the state's voters consider themselves independents, with the remainder splitting their allegiances between the two major parties.

The more I went over the speech, the more I thought about the reasoning behind it. Just as my colleagues couldn't understand how I could go ahead and switch, I couldn't understand how I could stay a Republican.

The budget and tax battles of the spring had brought home to me how wide a gulf had come to separate me from national Republican orthodoxy. While I thought we should use much of the surplus for addressing pressing domestic spending needs, such as education and child care and health care, few of my Republican colleagues saw these as high priorities. This view was based on their belief that the best government is the least government, and that as many surplus dollars as possible should be returned to the taxpayer.

I understand that view, but do not subscribe to it. It seems to me that a healthy skepticism of government ought to be leavened with an appreciation for what it can do and for what people cannot do for themselves. As Franklin Roosevelt once remarked, "Better the occasional faults of a government that lives in a spirit of charity than the consistent omissions of a government frozen in the ice of its own indifference."

Low-wage and even middle-class working parents simply cannot afford decent child care, yet research is making it abundantly clear that these early years in a child's life are both critical and largely irretrievable. Every other industrialized nation fully furnishes such care as part of the public school system. In our country, state and local governments are forced to bear ever larger costs for educating our children with special needs because the federal government has never made good on its promise to fund 40 percent of the costs of special education. And without a prodigious investment of additional funds, we will never help the more than 40 million Americans who lack health insurance.

This is an argument I can make to my constituents in Vermont and the vast majority will agree that we should invest more in our children, even if it means forgoing a share of a tax cut. Indeed, it is exactly the argument I made to Vermont voters in the fall of 2000 when I ran for reelection and won close to two-thirds of their votes. But for many of my Republican colleagues in Washington, this argument makes no sense. Throughout the spring, as I voiced my concerns in Republican meetings, I met with rolled eyes of disbelief more often than nodding heads of agreement.

I was a tangle of emotions on the flight home to Vermont. The tug of war between my allegiance to my friends in the Senate and remaining true to my own beliefs yielded no clear victor. I was beat, my emotions were still raw, and my thoughts were still somewhat unsettled.

But as the plane began its descent above the Champlain Valley into the familiar hills of Vermont, I knew the next day I would break with the party I had supported throughout my adult life. My first allegiance had to be not to my colleagues, but to my constituents and my conscience. The makeup of the Senate is not created by national referendum, but by thirty-three or so individual races in very different states every two years. As I had made clear in my Senate campaign six years before, my contract was not with America, but with Vermont.

I had tried to effect change within the party. I had tried to accommodate my beliefs to the party as a whole. I had tried to be fair to those with whom I had formed friendships over the decades. And I had tried to balance my decision against the impact it would have on my colleagues, my family, and my staff, many of whom would soon be thrown out of work. But in the end, I had to be true to what I thought was right, and leave the consequences to sort themselves out in the days ahead.

THAT frequent recurrence to fundamental principles, and a firm adherence to justice, moderation, temperance, industry and frugality, are absolutely necessary to preserve the blessings of liberty, and keep government free. The people ought, therefore, to pay particular attention to these points, in the choice of officers and representatives, and have a right to exact a due and constant regard to them, from their legislators and magistrates.

DECLARATION OF THE RIGHTS OF
THE INHABITANTS OF THE STATE OF VERMONT
JULY 8, 1777

TWO

Point of No Return

THE DAYS leading up to my decision had been a swirl of meetings, sleepless nights, and tough conversations with my family and senior staff. I am normally pretty open with people close to me when faced with an important political decision. My chief of staff, Susan Russ, has been with me for over two decades, while my staff director on the Health and Education Committee, Mark Powden, has worked for me nearly as long. I knew I could put absolute trust in them.

But my decision to break from the party caught them unawares. I had been mulling my growing discontent with the direction of the party throughout the spring. The party as a whole saw the election of President George W. Bush and the thin grasp Republicans maintained on the House and Senate as a wonderful opportunity to change the direction of government fundamentally. I did, too, but only because I was hopeful that we could, as the President had promised, change the tone of Washington and escape the poisonous relationship that had grown up between the Clinton Administration and Republicans in Congress.

Instead, the Bush Administration headed down the very same path that the new Clinton Administration had trod eight years earlier, taking a slim margin as a mandate and attempting to reward its political base with a largely partisan budget. President Bush publicly drew a line in the sand—whatever else happened, the budget must contain $1.6 trillion in tax cuts over the next ten years. Privately, the White House made clear that any Republican who thought otherwise was morally or mentally deficient.

Without question, this budget fight was a critical one, and not just because it was the first test of the Bush Administration. In an effort to rein in and better coordinate federal spending, Congress passed the Budget Act in 1974, a year when the entire federal budget deficit amounted to $6 billion. Today, that amount is almost a rounding error in a nearly $2 trillion budget. But as the stakes have risen in the budget process, the efficacy of the Budget Act has shrunk.

During the last few years of the Clinton Administration, budgets had become increasingly irrelevant. Since the budget is merely a blueprint for Congress and does not need to be signed into law by the President, Republicans crafted one partisan document after another. They would be passed amidst howls from the Democrats. But almost no one believed they would be observed in the late stages of the appropriations process in the fall, the so-called end game, when tens of billions of dollars would be added to whatever budget had been adopted in the spring. President Clinton's proposed budgets, which perennially called for the same familiar and unachievable budgetary savings, were greeted with Republican howls and equal measures of incredulity.

The election of President Bush had changed the dynamic considerably. Instead of greeting the President's budget submission with derision, Republicans acted as if it bordered on the divine. For the first time since the Eisenhower Administration, Republicans found themselves in control of both Houses of Congress and responsible for enacting the President's agenda. For Republicans serving in Congress, this was the first time in their careers they would have the opportunity to do so, and they were not about to let it slip from their grasp.

The stakes were even higher because no one could predict how long the political trifecta would last. A year before, the conventional wisdom in many circles had control of the House going to the Democrats and Al Gore defeating George Bush soundly. The conventional wisdom was not only wrong on both counts, it overestimated Republican strength in the Senate, where Paul Coverdell's tragic and early death had left the margin at 54 to 46.

Conservative senators who had won handily on the wave of reaction to the early Clinton Administration in 1994 found themselves in tough races. Four of them—Slade Gorton, Spence Abraham, John Ashcroft, and Bill Roth—lost in November of 2000, creating an evenly divided Senate, the first time an election had yielded such a result since 1881. At the same time these conservatives lost, moderate Republicans—Olympia Snowe in Maine, Lincoln Chafee in Rhode Island, and I—were able to win comfortably.

With Republicans' margin in the House having shrunk in three consecutive elections, with no margin in the Senate, and with many more seats to defend in 2002 than the Democrats, congressional Republicans knew they had to seize the moment. Compounding their plight was the slender Bush victory in the presidential race, and the historic tilt against the party holding the White House in off-year elections. Having watched the Democrats get wiped out in 1994, the first off-year election of the Clinton Administration, the Republicans had to fear a similar response from the voters in 2002.

If you are an orthodox Republican, how do you change the direction of government in two years' time? You cut off its oxygen, by cutting taxes as deeply and as widely as possible.

This had been the theory of the Reagan and first Bush Administrations, at least in part. But the real hammer on federal spending policy through the 1980s and most of the 1990s had been the deficit. From the $6 billion deficit in 1974 at the time of the enactment of the Budget Act, deficits had mushroomed to a record $290 billion under President George H. W. Bush. The national debt rose from $344 billion in 1974, to $3.433 trillion in 1994.

Interest costs ballooned, and spending on important domestic priorities shrank. In fiscal year 2000, spending on domestic discretionary programs—everything from controlling air traffic to feeding the zebras at the National Zoo—represented only 17 percent of the federal budget. Twenty years earlier, it had stood at 25 percent. Education, which was at the center of presidential campaigns in the year 2000, commands a tiny share of the federal budget. The entire Department of Education receives just 2 percent of all federal spending.

Although the end game produced some increased spending, the overall fiscal picture brightened considerably as the 1990s came to a close. A combination of factors—the budget agreement of 1990, the tax hike of 1993, some spending restraint by Congress throughout—produced the first federal surplus of my entire career in 1998.

Republicans and Democrats will argue as long as they have breath as to who gets the credit. Frankly, the real credit goes to neither party; rather, it goes to the workers and entrepreneurs who generated the longest economic expansion in our history. Revenues surged throughout the decade. The Congressional Budget Office was continually increasing its estimates of federal revenues. Money was coming into the Treasury faster than Congress and the President could dream up and agree upon ways to send it back out.

Deficits were no longer the hammer that would keep spending in check as they had through the Reagan, Bush, and Clinton Administrations. While the surpluses of 1998, 1999, and 2000 were novel, by the time the second George Bush came into office, most of Congress believed the surpluses were here to stay for the foreseeable future if we didn't screw things up too badly.

As often happens in politics, changed circumstances caused the parties to change places. Democrats, who normally would like nothing better than to spend whatever money was available, suddenly began sounding like small-town bankers in their fealty to paying down the national debt. Republicans, who had taken exactly this approach in the face of the previous administration, just as suddenly decided that we really shouldn't pay down the debt too much or too quickly.

Both sides were shaping their economic arguments to suit their larger political ends. Republicans wanted to shrink the size of government by cutting off revenues. Without deficits hanging over our debates, they knew that a dollar raised could be a dollar spent. Democrats knew that any dollar not raised could never be spent. Once taxes were cut, it could be political suicide to try to increase them in any significant way.

And so was the stage set for the budget and tax debates of spring 2001. There was precious little contemplation of where our national needs lay, and little or no examination of any long-term consequences of our actions. Our decisions often seemed driven by a simple and almost instinctive approach to government, as something to be revered or reviled, nurtured or neutered.

I found myself out of step with both approaches. It seemed to me that you could have it both ways, a substantial tax cut directed at helping working Americans, and substantially increased spending on the sorts of things that both presidential candidates had talked about in the fall.

This was not some new revelation. It was exactly what I had campaigned on in the fall of 2000. As I had put it in the text of a speech to the Burlington Rotary Club in October 1999:

The surplus has created a whole new set of headaches, as some of my colleagues want to devote it to either a new spending spree or unsustainable tax cuts. I disagree, and here is what I would do with the surplus.

First, we should set aside any surpluses in Social Security and Medicare into a lockbox for each. What this means is that more than half the surplus—over $2.7 trillion—will be used to pay down the debt, reduce interest costs, and give us some room for borrowing when the baby boom retires.

I'd split the remainder—about $1.8 trillion—into thirds. The first third should be set aside for both the expected and the unexpected: expiring tax provisions like the R&D tax credit and employer-provided educational assistance, natural disasters and other emergencies, and changes in the economic forecast.

The second third should be spent on important national priorities like fully funding special education and providing a drug benefit under Medicare.

The final third should be given back to the taxpayers in the form of both targeted and broad-based tax cuts, like repealing the marriage penalty and providing limited estate tax relief for farms and small businesses. The federal government is taking a higher share out of the economy since 1944 when we were invading Hitler's Europe. We need to give some back to the taxpayers who earned it.

At the time, I thought this speech was a pretty good statement of my views and those of moderate Republicans generally. But as the surplus grew, Republicans seemed to move away from my position while the Democrats came toward it.

The only problem with my campaign formulation was that it became very close to what the Democrats settled upon as their approach four months later. The senior Democrat on the Budget Committee, Kent Conrad, stated on February 15:

I have proposed a budget plan to protect Social Security and Medicare, reserving every penny of those trust fund surpluses for those programs. My plan would then divide the non–Social Security, non-Medicare surplus into equal thirds of $900 billion: one third for tax cuts; one third for high priority domestic programs such as health care, including a prescription drug benefit, education, defense and agriculture; and one third to reduce the long-term debt created by our obligations to fund Social Security and Medicare.

What had happened in the eighteen months or so since Republicans had so proudly trumpeted their $792 billion tax cut over ten years? The surplus kept growing like a welcome weed as the economy continued to generate revenues at a furious pace, full employment led to reduced demand for government services, and inflation, especially in the critical area of health care, remained modest.

Without much discussion or debate, Republicans as a whole decided that virtually all the new funds would be dedicated to tax cuts, and almost none would go to reversing the decline of domestic discretionary spending. But how our children lag behind their international peers strikes me as a bigger long-term threat to our national security and stability than the rate of taxation paid on multimillion-dollar estates. In my mind, the education we give to all of our children is far more important than the size of the fortunes left to a fortunate few.

In April, the Senate began its consideration of the budget for the upcoming fiscal year. Since the evenly divided Budget Committee could not agree to a budget resolution by the usual majority vote, the budget came to the floor of the Senate for the first time without the support of a majority of the committee. The problem for the Republican leadership and the White House was that the budget lacked a majority on the Senate floor as well.

In the first few days of February, I tried to signal my concern about the size of the proposed tax cut, which was double what I had campaigned for and a direct threat to increased spending for education and health care. I bluntly told a reporter for CNN that as far as the $1.6 trillion tax cut was concerned, "right now, the size of it, I think, is too high, so I would vote to cut it." My staff privately conveyed to the White House that it should not base its budget strategy on the assumption that it would hold all fifty Senate Republican votes.

Through March and into early April, the pressure increased on me and my fellow wayward Republican, Senator Lincoln Chafee of Rhode Island, to support the President's call for $1.6 trillion in tax cuts. But tax cuts had not been what animated the people of Vermont I talked to on the campaign trail in the fall. They seemed far more concerned with meeting human needs.

One day I was invited to Majority Leader Trent Lott's office on the second floor of the Capitol for a discussion with him, Assistant Majority Leader Don Nickles, Budget Committee Chairman Pete Domenici, and Chuck Grassley on what it would take to get my support for the budget. I listed one area after another where I saw the need for greater investment, from early education to math and science instruction to coming to grips with the nursing shortage in our country.

I could see my Republican colleagues drift further and further away. When I mentioned the need for nearly $200 billion in increased spending on education for disabled students over the next ten years, Trent asked if I meant for it to be guaranteed. I answered yes. As the meeting concluded, Don Nickles left the room cursing me in a very loud stage whisper.

My colleagues had trouble believing I was serious, and I had trouble making yet more empty promises on special education. While I would not have had the audacity to expect close to $200 billion for special education a year or two before, it seemed to me that, in the context of a $1.6 trillion tax cut, this was not an unreasonable request. In the days that followed this meeting, I decided to winnow down my list of spending priorities to this one.

———

It seemed to me the most fruitful avenue, in part because it was the most Republican.

Throughout the Clinton Administration, Republicans had argued that rather than spending money on a host of new programs, such as class size reduction or school construction, Congress and the White House ought to focus on fulfilling the promise we made in 1975 to fund 40 percent of the costs of educating disabled children.

A quarter century ago, the civil rights movement of the 1950s and 1960s had spawned activism across various segments of society, including disabled Americans. By 1975, courts across the country were finding that schools could no longer warehouse children with disabilities, sometimes literally putting them in closets, but that state and federal constitutions obliged schools to provide all children with a free and appropriate education.

One of the few benefits of having arrived on the Democratic Watergate tsunami was rapid career advancement for freshmen Republicans. There were so few of us in the House that I instantly became the senior Republican on the education subcommittee charged with overseeing the education of disabled children. Responding to the courts' decisions and litigation in over half the states, Congress in 1975 enacted the Education of the Handicapped Act, which has since been renamed the Individuals with Disabilities Education Act, or IDEA. What we tried to do was to set rules of the road for schools and parents to follow so as to provide a fair balance between the needs of disabled students and the resources of local school districts.

At the time, we realized a burden would be placed on the state and local governments. Yet we did not want to write a blank check, either. The compromise we arrived at assumed that state and local governments would pay the basic cost of educating disabled children just as they would any other child. We thought the cost of educating a disabled child would be about twice that of a nondisabled child, and committed the federal government to pay 40 percent of the national average per pupil expenditure for each disabled child's education. If it fulfilled its commitment, the federal government would shoulder one dollar in five of the total educational costs for students with disabilities, not four in ten as some people may believe. Even with full federal funding, state and local governments would have ample reason to watch their spending.

IDEA has been a great success in providing the basic constitutional right of an education to our disabled children. Like any other law, it is not perfect, and every five years or so Congress has stepped in to make adjustments. We still have more work to do in improving the law. Too much time and effort is wasted on adjudicating issues, and recent evidence shows a tremendous over-identification of minority students that we must rectify.

But the biggest failure is that the federal government does not fund its share. Instead of 40 percent of the costs that Congress promised in 1975, the best we have ever done is about 15 percent, which is where we stand today. Republicans can rightly claim credit for the tremendous increase in IDEA spending over the past five years. But we are still well short of where we need and promised to be.

Every dollar that the federal government fails to provide must be supplied by state and local government. For towns that are straining to pass a school budget, this federal failure risks fueling resentment against families that already have enough to deal with in raising a child with special needs. In small towns such as we have in Vermont, a single child or two with severe disabilities can have a significant impact on a school's budget. And a higher share of funding must come from more regressive sources such as the property tax.

Which is exactly why we have a federal government—to spread these costs across all of society. I don't know a person alive who doesn't agree that we as a society have a responsibility to educate all of our children. Indeed, over the past several years the Senate has cast one unanimous symbolic vote after another to fully fund IDEA. But when I began to press my colleagues on making these promises real in the early months of 2001, most of my Republican colleagues recoiled.

The reaction was not universal. Senator Chuck Hagel, a conservative Republican from Nebraska, early on grasped that fulfilling our commitment under IDEA did not represent new spending so much as it did taking over some of the burden from local governments. But his brand of independence and common sense is too rare a commodity.

In March and early April, I made my case to the Republican leadership and to the White House that we should triple the amount of money we spend on IDEA over the course of a few years so that we would finally meet the 40 percent commitment we made in 1975. At the same time, I thought that it was critical that we convert it to a so-called mandatory spending program, on a par with Social Security or student loans.

As it stands today, IDEA is a discretionary program, forced to compete every year for funding with hundreds of other worthy education, health, and social services programs. The results of this twenty-six-year experiment are obvious. Disabled children are not a potent enough lobby to receive their due. Given the size of the tax cut, the increases in defense spending that the Bush Administration will seek, and the aging of the baby boom generation, there will be tremendous pressure on domestic spending over the next decade.

I was never sure that the Republican leadership believed that I was serious, even though I had always done my best to be straight with them about where I would be on a given issue. And I think the White House may have been relying on its ability, or Trent Lott's, to turn me around. But I was quite serious, and my staff and I tried to make that point repeatedly so they would not mistake my intentions.

Perhaps they had some inkling. They worked assiduously to win the votes of moderate Democrats for the President's $1.6 trillion tax cut. Indeed, at times their interest in working with me seemed inversely proportional to the success they felt they were having with Democratic Senators Ben Nelson of Nebraska, Bob Torricelli of New Jersey, or John Breaux of Louisiana. They weren't having much. They had early on won the support of Senator Zell Miller, a Democrat from Georgia, but having lost my vote and that of Linc Chafee, they were down one vote. Every Senator had leverage—we knew it, and they knew it.

The White House had painted itself into a political corner. It had defined the $1.6 trillion figure as the difference between success and failure. And since the President's advisers felt this would set the tone for the entire Bush Administration, they were unwilling to deviate from it. As a result, my argument that we should scale back the tax cut and devote the funds to special education fell on largely deaf ears in the weeks leading up to consideration of the budget in the first week of April. The $1.6 trillion figure had become the Holy Grail for the White House. I was something of an infidel.

As the day of reckoning arrived, the Republican leadership and the White House had not found the Democratic vote they needed, and they came back to me with a newfound interest in reaching an agreement on special education funding. As one of Senator Lott's staff remarked at the time, although he had thought my demand was so ambitious as to price me out of the political marketplace, it turned out it might not be.

The debate on the budget for fiscal year 2002 began on the afternoon of Monday, April 2. The beginning of such a debate is usually consumed by set pieces on the floor of the Senate, as both parties make outsized claims for the good or harm that will flow from the budget at hand. Behind the scenes, I was working the phones and walking the halls to try to secure the IDEA funding.

That morning I had met with Senator Lott and by the end of our meeting I thought I had secured agreement to reduce the tax cut to $1.4 trillion, fully fund IDEA at a cost of $180 billion, and hold it when the Senate ironed out its differences with the House in a conference committee. My optimism was short lived.

About an hour later I met with Senate Budget Committee Chairman Pete Domenici in the so-called Marble Room, the Senators' private lobby just off the Senate floor. I did my best to persuade Pete of the importance of the issue, spending about ten minutes laying out in detail the history of IDEA, our commitment, its importance, and the possibilities within the budget. When I finished, Pete clasped his hands together, rocked forward, and exclaimed, "God, Jeffords, you are so damn passionate about this thing, aren't you!" His staff jumped in with a new offer, seemingly no better than the last. I said I'd look at it.

Pete is a straight shooter, and he has always been fair to me. But what he proposed was a hybrid plan that in my estimation could not work. The current discretionary spending program for IDEA would continue, but layered on top of it would be a new mandatory program.

This solved one of Pete's biggest problems by keeping the cost of the new mandatory spending program lower, but it created a practical problem for me. The members of the appropriations committee could almost be counted on to reduce discretionary funds for special education as new mandatory money became available. The net effect would be no effect at all. When Pete called me at noon I told him this, even while I agreed I would likely support him on the procedural votes made necessary by his inability to get a committee majority in support of the bill.

Later in the day, my legislative director, Ken Connolly, was trying to find me in the Capitol and mistakenly walked in on a budget meeting under way in Senator Lott's office. While there, he asked Senator Domenici's staff about the status of our negotiations. The meeting was breaking up, and as Domenici rose from the table, his staff relayed the question. Not recognizing Ken, Pete replied, "What Jeffords wants is crazy. He'll never get it. I'm done dealing with him." Lott's chief of staff tried to signal to Domenici that he was speaking to a Jeffords staffer, but Pete waved him off by saying "I don't care who heard that."

A little after five that afternoon I met in the Vice President's Room off the Senate floor with Vice President Cheney. I had served with Dick in the House when he was the Minority Whip and I was the senior Republican on the Education and Labor Committee. Our relations were cordial, though we were not particularly close. The Vice President wanted to try again on the hybrid proposal that I had rejected earlier in the day in my conversation with Senator Domenici.

The meeting was inconclusive, but I started to get the sense that the administration was simply trying to find a way to survive the next few days, promising me something, almost anything, and then throwing it overboard once it reached the conference committee that would resolve differences between the House- and Senate-passed bills.

About an hour after I left the meeting with Cheney, I put an outline of my bottom line on a piece of paper and gave it to Pete Domenici on the Senate floor. I needed full mandatory funding, and the White House and Senate leadership must support both it and the necessary authorizing language that would effect the change throughout the entire legislative process.

It continually amazes me how people's perceptions can be so starkly different. What seemed to me to be a simple restatement of what I had been talking about for weeks was greeted by at least some in the White House as an eleventh-hour apostasy. The idea that the President would actually sign the legislation needed to make the funding real was seen as a new, unreasonable demand.

Given the White House reaction, I was immediately grateful that the issue had been joined. It only added to my suspicion and made me more careful. I wondered whether the White House thought I was after nothing more than a symbolic victory. I didn't want or need any more feel-good press releases on IDEA. I wanted exactly what I had said I wanted—full, guaranteed spending for IDEA.

The next morning I met with Senator Domenici in the Republican cloakroom off the Senate floor to discuss IDEA funding yet again. He had consulted with the administration and was prepared to offer $153 billion over ten years in mandatory spending, which would come out of the so-called contingency fund rather than from the tax cut. He said he would do everything he could to hold it through the conference, but could make no promises. The slight reduction in spending would come from unspecified reforms in a few years' time. The question came up as to whether this was the same hybrid proposal that had been discussed earlier, and the response was that it was not, that it was unclear how such a hybrid proposal could ever work.

Of particular interest to me was that this proposal was characterized as a "pure add." In the argot of congressional budgeting, this means that every dollar spent on IDEA via this new mandatory spending would free up a dollar in discretionary spending. This was extremely important to me for two reasons. First, members of the appropriations committees are always loath to give up control over spending. It seemed to me that I might win their support if they lost authority over IDEA but controlled the same amount of funding. If they lost funding as well, they might well oppose me, as a few of them had in an earlier effort the year before.

But the second and more important reason was that part of my aim in shifting IDEA to mandatory funding was to free up funds in the discretionary budget for other purposes, such as improving education generally, and especially early education.

The Bush Administration's budget had sent mixed messages on early education, canceling out funding for one program while proposing a new initiative to improve reading among young children. The quality of the education we provide to our three- and four- and five-year-olds is often abysmal. Children who arrive at school behind their peers have terrible difficulty catching up.

And we have done far too little to help our children to catch up with their peers around the world. Our children rank at the bottom of international math rankings, and we do not do much better in science. Nearly two-thirds of inner-city children cannot read at the basic level as measured by the National Assessment of Educational Progress. We must do a better job of educating not only our disabled children, but all our children.

I left the meeting with Pete Domenici guardedly optimistic. I could live with the reduced funding if the rest of the agreement was as I understood it. But discussions over the past few days had been sufficiently turbulent that I was not going to believe it too quickly.

Sure enough, in the middle of the afternoon I met with Pete in the Vice President's Room, where he delivered the news that we had no deal. Some of the more conservative Republicans in our caucus had balked at the idea of a "new" mandatory spending program, overlooking the fact that it was already very much in place in every school district in the country, paid for by state and local property taxes and other funds.

I didn't fault Pete Domenici. He had the unenviable task of trying to juggle half a dozen balls while trying to manage a bill on the floor. I was pushing for more education spending at the same time as other groups of Senators were pushing for more spending on agriculture, defense, and a host of other areas. It did Pete no good to secure my vote and lose five others.

In the wake of our meeting, it looked like my efforts had played out and that either another vote had been found from the Democratic ranks or the budget would fail by a vote. I spoke with Senator John Breaux of Louisiana, a moderate Democrat who had been trying to marshal a small band of centrist Senators around a compromise budget, and told him I would likely join him at a press conference he had planned for the following afternoon with a few other Democratic Senators and Senator Chafee.

Although Senator Lott's chief of staff indicated that night that they still wanted to talk, the next morning passed without a word. Just after midday I spoke with Chuck Hagel, who thought I should give it more time, but I wasn't sure time would change much of anything. But it's not in my nature to refuse people, so when I was asked to meet with Senator Domenici in his Capitol hideaway at two that afternoon I agreed to do so, asking that the White House be involved as well.

Pete and everyone else involved with the budget knew

I was planning to attend the Breaux press conference at two forty-five that afternoon, so he didn't waste time getting to the point. Neither did I. I knew my problem was with the White House, not him, so I was surprised that at the outset of our meeting no one from the White House was present.

Pete and I spoke for a few minutes before he left to get the President's representatives into the room. Strangely enough, though the halls were full of the key White House staff in these critical days of the budget, finding them proved to be a difficult task. About ten minutes later, Pete returned and told me that the White House staff was on their way but that he had to return to the floor.

Ten more minutes passed. It was now two-thirty, just fifteen minutes before the Breaux press conference was to begin. Finally a representative of the Vice President and a White House legislative liaison staffer appeared. They informed me that the Vice President had "just two minutes ago" authorized senior White House staff to sit down and see if they could work things out. I was informed that they were on their way. Asked if they had anything new to offer, they said no, but repeated that more senior policy staff were on their way. We waited, with growing frustration and rising anger.

As the clock ticked, it became clearer and clearer to me that the White House was playing a game of stall ball, by having lower level staff keep talking with me until the Breaux press conference had passed, thus stealing some of his thunder and buying a few critical hours to figure out the next maneuver.

Senator Breaux's staff was understandably exercised. His press secretary called my press aide Erik Smulson on his cell phone at about two forty-five, wondering how long Senator Breaux would have to keep telling bad jokes before beginning the press conference. Erik, who was standing outside in the hallway between the Domenici and Lott offices, couldn't tell her whether I'd even attend.

Inside Pete's office, with the Breaux press conference already under way, my staff and I were finally forced to ask the White House staff to leave the room. All of us had come to the same conclusion: The White House was stalling for time to scuttle my appearance with Breaux and had no intention of changing its position on IDEA spending.

I wasn't sure what I should do. Susan Russ cut through the clutter and asked who best represented what I thought was the right approach to the budget. Without hesitation, I answered the moderates headed up by John Breaux.

With that we were on the move. Susan went across the hallway to inform Senator Lott's staff of my decision. Erik went to summon the elevator, signaling with a thumb's up to the press gathered at the public end of the off-limits corridor that I was heading up to the centrists' press conference.

Fifteen minutes late, I went up the tiny elevator, twentieth-century technology squeezed in a former ventilation shaft from the nineteenth. In the third-floor press gallery, the news conference was under way. I had had no intention of making a dramatic entrance, but the result was unavoidable. If the Democrats held their ranks, Linc Chafee and I represented the votes to defeat the President's budget. The usually jaded press corps reacted with an audible gasp, Senator Breaux's press secretary with tears.

A huge smile broke out on John Breaux's face when he saw me. The White House would have to moderate its demands and abandon its strategy of ramming a budget through the Senate on a near party-line vote. And I had reached what I thought was the point of no return on the budget.

I concluded my remarks at the press conference with the observation that "I feel very comfortable here, first time in a while." Amidst the crowd's laughter, Senator

Chafee responded that "I feel comfortable that you're here, too." I regretted that I had not been successful in my goal of securing White House agreement for full funding of IDEA, but I had no regrets for supporting a tax cut that might leave room to make that goal still possible.

I SOLEMNLY swear, by the ever living God [or affirm in the presence of Almighty God], that whenever I am called to give my vote or suffrage, touching any matter that concerns the State of Vermont, I will do it so, as in my conscience, I shall judge will most conduce to the best good of the same, as established by the constitution, without fear or favor of any man.

VERMONT FREEMAN'S OATH
JULY 8, 1777

THREE

A Short Walk Across the Aisle

IN THE midst of the press conference, the Senate began to vote on a key amendment of the entire budget debate. It was offered by Senator Tom Harkin of Iowa, another colleague who entered Congress with me in the Watergate class of 1974. But even though he represented the same state as Chuck Grassley and had entered the House the same year, the two were very different. Tom is the prototypical Watergate baby, a populist Democrat, as liberal as Chuck is conservative.

The Harkin amendment proposed to knock the tax cut back by $450 billion, spending $250 billion on IDEA and other education and training programs and applying $200 billion to debt service. It was just the sort of approach I had been advocating in my discussions with the White House and the Republican leadership.

Since I had struck out trying to win the support of the administration for greater education spending, I cast my vote for the Harkin amendment without hesitation. Combined with the votes of Republicans Lincoln Chafee and Arlen Specter of Pennsylvania, the Harkin amendment was on its way to adoption when I left the Senate chamber and headed to a meeting already under way on the education bill that we had voted out of the education committee a month before.

The meeting was one of several that took place among a group of senators that Trent Lott and Senate Democratic Leader Tom Daschle had informally designated to try to work out as many areas of agreement as possible. The education bill was slated to be the next order of business following completion of the budget. We met in a room on the third floor of the Capitol in what used to be the Senate Library, a beautiful room lined with bookshelves and alcoves that provide a sweeping view of the Mall.

I had been there only a few minutes when Senator Lott's staff summoned me for a meeting in his hideaway office down a few hallways. I knew the purpose, to turn me around on the Harkin vote. Given the vehemence of the White House and the Republican leadership in their quest for the full tax cut, I joshed with my education staffer, Sherry Kaiman, that it had been nice knowing her.

I know Senator Lott's hideaway office very well. It was the place where I had spent an hour almost every Tuesday and Thursday morning over the past five years practicing with my fellow Singing Senators—Trent Lott, Larry Craig of Idaho, and John Ashcroft of Missouri. We had come together quite by accident, and seemed destined to disprove the maxim that practice makes perfect. I was easily the weakest link. Naturally a baritone, I was singing first tenor and stretching my range, but our group had always struck me as more about fun and fellowship than forsaking Capitol Hill for Nashville.

That night's meeting had an altogether different tone. One by one, the President's senior staff drifted into the room, and soon we began discussing how we might reach an agreement that would deliver them the tax cut and me special education funding. We clearly came from very different positions. I think they viewed me as disloyal to the President, while I saw myself as loyal to Vermonters and a central campaign promise I had made them.

We went back and forth, seeming at times to talk past one another. The President's head of congressional relations, Nick Calio, made appeals to past support and spoke darkly of the future if I opposed the President. At one point, another of Bush's senior advisers asked me what their incentive would be to deal with me if I proposed to reduce the tax cut below $1.6 trillion. "How about educating children?" I responded, not intending to be sarcastic but probably coming off that way.

Apparently, the White House staff was unaware that I had already voted for the Harkin amendment, because midway through the meeting they learned of it and said that if my vote stood, there was nothing more to discuss. The vote, which is normally scheduled to take place over a very loose fifteen minutes, was held open for what seemed like forever as we haggled down the hall from the Senate gallery. It finally ended, as did our fruitless meeting.

I left the meeting thinking that really we had passed the point of no return, but again I was wrong. Trent had cast his vote on the side of the Democrats to preserve the parliamentary option of voting again on the Harkin amendment. Under the rules of the Senate, any senator on the winning side of a question can move to reconsider it. By voting with the Democrats, Trent could beat the Harkin amendment if he could turn two votes around. The White House promised to put a new proposal on paper, and I agreed to meet with them later that evening.

Ever the optimist, I thought the White House might finally make some proposal for full mandatory spending. I was mistaken. The next meeting produced a rehash of the proposal Vice President Cheney had made two days before. Not only did it involve the flawed hybrid funding of Monday's proposal, but it would displace, not add to, discretionary funds. Moreover, the President would not agree to any mandatory funding unless an unspecified set of reforms recommended by a yet-to-be-named commission were adopted a few years hence.

The political uncertainty surrounding the White House's proposal was immense. It had taken us three years and several false starts to reach agreement on modest IDEA reforms in 1997. There was no knowing what the makeup of the commission would be, what it would recommend, whether it would be policy I could support, and regardless of my support, whether it could command a consensus in Congress. That was at least four ifs too many to attach to funding of a program that was long overdue. I certainly thought and think that IDEA can and should be improved to serve children better, but I don't know why we would want to add new and perhaps unachievable conditions before we fulfilled our decades-old promise.

Compounding my concern were the stark realities of the budget. The tax cuts would begin to kick in right away, and an increase in military spending would be not too far behind. Even assuming a somewhat miraculous legislative path for IDEA reforms over the next two years, by the time we achieved any agreement on policy, the money to fund it might well have evaporated.

I broke off talks with the White House that night and thought we were done. But the next morning, Thursday, I got a call from Trent asking me to meet with him and Vice President Cheney during the vote scheduled to occur at 9:45 A.M. While nothing had changed overnight, I felt I should hear them out one more time. Once more I went to the Vice President's Room, which by now had been dubbed "the Torture Chamber." Once more I repeated that I could not support the tax cut without guaranteed funding for special education, and that the White House proposal had too many loopholes for my satisfaction.

The Thursday morning meeting in the Vice President's Room produced nothing new. If anything, we moved further apart, as the White House, no doubt echoing my demand for clarity, laid out all the procedural and other votes they expected me to cast in return for their rather flimsy offer on special education funding.

We were done. Late that morning I sent the Vice President a note expressing my regret that we could not reach an agreement. In the sometimes jarring world of scheduling in the Senate, I then kept a lunch date with my son Leonard, where we honored Scotland and one of its most famous sons, Sean Connery. Started by Trent, the now-annual Tartan Day celebrates Scotland's fight for independence and contributions to America. Trent had come to know Leonard from Singing Senators events, and the two of them got along well. Dressed in kilt and full regalia, Trent convinced Leonard to push me to accept half a loaf in the budget negotiations. It was a bizarre lunch. Although it was a hot day outside, it was pretty chilly for me among my Republican colleagues inside the Capitol.

Early that afternoon, I took Liz's good advice and we went to our house in Washington. I was frustrated and angry, as was she. What I had been seeking seemed so clearly right to me, and so clearly consistent with furthering education in our country, yet I had failed to secure it.

The next day brought an end to the week and the budget debate. On Friday the Senate adopted a truly bipartisan budget with sixty-five votes, which included a tax cut of $1.25 trillion. By almost any reckoning, the President had achieved a tremendous victory. He had won the vast majority of the tax cuts he had sought, and he had done so with the support of fifteen Democratic Senators, exactly the kind of governing coalition he would need with his narrow mandate and the even narrower margin in the Senate. Instead, given the inflexibility of the White House, it was treated almost as a loss by political observers. The self-congratulatory statements from the other end of Pennsylvania Avenue sounded hollow in their satisfaction.

Before we had even completed action on the budget, hints had emerged from the White House and elsewhere that I would be forced to pay a political price for bucking the President on the budget bill. One anonymous senior Republican source was quoted remarking that "the White House is not giving specifics, but there's a one- or two-year plan to punish him for his behavior. And it's stuff that may hurt him, but stuff that's not going to draw a significant amount of attention. So they're going to get him."

After the budget was voted on, the head of Vermont's Associated Press bureau, Chris Graff, interviewed me by phone for a weekend public television news program. At the end of his questions, he asked me about possible reprisals. My response contained what I thought was a statement of the obvious, that it was a short walk across the aisle.

SOON THE stories in the press started to get more specific, suggesting that my vote on the budget would lead to reprisals against the dairy farmers of the Northeast. Whether these stories came from the White House or the milk processors who stood to gain from the farmers' loss, I still don't know.

With the break for Easter and the distractions of organizing an evenly divided Senate, it took the House and Senate conferees about a month to reach agreement on a final budget blueprint. It took so long in part because the conferees had to divine the combination of spending and tax cuts that would yield majority votes in the House and Senate. Lower the tax cut number too far, and conservatives in both bodies would bolt. Too much in the way of tax cuts, and the handful of Democrats needed would desert.

While we waited for the conferees to complete action on the budget bill, the Senate took up the reauthorization of our nation's elementary and secondary education programs. This bill, which I had drafted with my colleagues on the education committee and which had been adopted by the committee on a unanimous vote, could represent a remarkable achievement or an unmitigated disaster.

While the federal government's role in elementary and secondary education is financially small, supplying about 7 percent of all funds, it can have a tremendous impact, particularly in the poorer schools where most federal funds are focused. The bill debated and adopted by the Senate, like its companion in the House, will substantially alter the federal role by insisting on far greater accountability from states, school districts, and individual schools, while providing them with much greater flexibility in many respects.

The bill also embraces the President's early reading initiative, which is designed to help children acquire the basic building blocks needed to become proficient readers. This is tremendously important, both in its own right and in reducing the need to steer children who have reading difficulties into special education.

That's the good news. But there are two pieces of bad news. First, we run the very real risk of setting the bar of achievement so high that *all* schools will be labeled failures. This of course helps no one. But so many of our deliberations to date had been so divorced from real world experience as to astonish me after all my time in Congress. President Bush, to his great credit, understands this and so far has ignored the ill-founded criticism directed his way. Second, wherever we set the bar, it is unlikely that the funds will flow from the federal government in anywhere near the amounts that would be necessary to ensure success. Every dollar in tax cuts is a dollar unavailable for education. On this point I cannot be so complimentary to the President.

The White House and I had started out a little rocky on this legislation, as the administration was wedded throughout February to a strategy of ignoring the deliberations in the committee and concentrating its attention on the House and the Senate floor. This seemed unwise in my view, as the committee could, would, and did give the President most of what he sought. Ignoring the Democrats and most of the Republicans on the education committee struck me as an odd way to go about the bipartisan education reform the President claimed to seek.

The last week of April was filled with events designed to promote the education bill. The first event used by the White House that week to highlight the issue was the announcement of the National Teacher of the Year on Monday, April 23. The award requires a rigorous screening process and really does recognize exceptional individuals and all their high-achieving colleagues across the country.

This year's honoree is no exception. Michele Forman, a high school history teacher from Salisbury, Vermont, is a remarkable person. She puts in long hours, and more important, she inspires her students with her own infectious love of learning. I was so pleased that she had won that I was eager to attend the White House ceremony in her honor and was fully expecting an invitation. This was the first time in the fifty-one years of the competition that a Vermonter was to be honored, and for a small state like ours it was very big news. When no invitation was forthcoming my scheduler, Trecia McEvoy, called the White House and was informed that no Members of Congress would be joining the President at the White House ceremony.

I left it at that. Clearly it was Ms. Foreman's day, and whether I attended or not mattered little. I got a chance to visit with her and her family and Vermont Education Commissioner David Wolk for an hour in my office after the ceremony, and chalked it up to the inexperience of a new White House. But I couldn't help wondering if the lack of an invitation was designed to send a message. Members of Congress are routinely welcomed to these events, I was chairman of the education committee, and I was managing the President's education bill on the Senate floor.

As the press began to focus on the decision of the White House, the rationale put forward sounded a little thin. White House spokesman Ari Fleischer responded to press questions by saying that the reason we could not be invited was because of the space limitations. It was hard to stifle a laugh. As my fellow Vermont Senator, Pat Leahy, remarked of the tiny three-man Vermont delegation, "We could all ride down on a Razor scooter if we had to."

The event made me something of a martyr in Vermont. I tried to brush it off, but the press carried the story for days, showing yet again how dumb little mistakes can have outsized consequences. Ironically, instead of attending the White House event I fulfilled my previous commitment to make fundraising calls from the Republican Senatorial Committee on behalf of the President's Dinner, a big fundraising event designed to help Republican candidates in 2002.

Three days later, it was "Take Your Child to Work" day, and with eleven-year-old Russell Powden in tow I traveled to Senator Lott's office for a meeting on education and taxes. While Russell chatted with his dad and other staff in Lott's outer office, in Trent's conference room I was engaged in the most discouraging meeting I had ever had with him. He was concerned about the education bill and my failure to embrace all of the Republican positions, and saw my actions on tax cuts as utterly disloyal. I could not convince him otherwise.

I left the Lott office for a press conference with business leaders promoting the education bill, including strong testing provisions that give conservative Republicans heartburn.

For much of May, I managed the education bill on the floor of the Senate. The White House, meanwhile, tried to promote the bill and the importance of education generally, which had been such a successful issue for the President on the campaign trail the previous fall. This success was due in large part because the President is genuine in his commitment to education and education reform.

On May 9, the debate on the education bill was interrupted to consider the final conference agreement on the budget. In the end, the conferees had agreed to a tax cut of $1.35 trillion. Before the agreement came to a vote in the Senate, I sat down with Pete Domenici at two desks on the Senate floor. With a yellow sheet of paper in his hand, he outlined the broad concepts. He tried to reassure me that hundreds of billions of dollars in contingency funds over the next ten years could be available for education, but it was a far cry from what I had sought. Too many competing interests would lay claim to those funds before they ever reached our schools.

Not surprisingly, the tax cut put substantial pressure on any new spending for education. The agreement between the House and Senate conferees provided for a little more money for education in 2002, but no increase whatsoever in the years beyond. Meanwhile, the wealthiest Americans would receive substantial reductions in their tax burden.

I don't practice class warfare. I think the genius of the American system has been to encourage risk with reward. It's not surprising that a tax code that generates most of its revenues from the affluent will yield like benefits for them when scaled back. But it seemed to me that if close to $1.4 trillion could be found for tax cuts, some substantial amount could have been found for education.

For most Republicans, I was speaking a foreign language. A self-styled budget watchdog group with ties to the Republican leadership labeled me as "Porker of the Month" for my refusal to support the President's tax cut without increased spending on special education. Only in Washington, D.C., I suspect, is spending for educating disabled students across the nation considered a pork barrel project.

I voted against the budget agreement, but my disappointment was more profound than that one vote indicated. Here I was, the chairman of the Senate's education committee, at the outset of a new millennium, when knowledge was becoming more important to individual and national success, when our society was becoming more stratified in many ways, when a major reform of education was about to take place, and yet my party couldn't find any additional money to invest in education.

It was a bitter disappointment, and I knew then I needed to do something. I had no real idea just what to do, but in the next two weeks the answer would come.

To PURGE the Party organization of its reactionary and unfair elements, to focus its forces on the recognition of the youth of our nation, to prepare immediately an affirmative program —that is the demand which the Republican leadership of Vermont makes on the Republican leadership of the nation.

If that demand is not met, we must look elsewhere for an organization through which thoughtful and devoted Americans of North and South, East and West, can join together to work for the good of all.

OPEN LETTER TO THE REPUBLICAN
NATIONAL COMMITTEE, SENATOR GEORGE AIKEN
DECEMBER 4, 1937

FOUR

Coup of One

I WASN'T doing a very good job of disguising my feelings on the budget, perhaps from a lack of trying. On the last Friday of March, I traded calls all day with Senator Chris Dodd of Connecticut in an attempt to discuss an amendment on child care we were planning to offer to the budget the following week. Since we were both staying in town that weekend, we finally decided to meet in person.

Late that afternoon, when most Senators were on planes headed home and their staffs were breathing a collective sigh of relief, Dodd's office was dark, quiet, and relaxed. His walls were covered with pictures of old sailing ships. Above his fireplace in the Russell Building hung a portrait of Thomas More, who Chris likes to point out is the only lawyer and politician to become a saint—at a cost, I might add, that those of us with the same credentials would rather avoid.

For close to an hour we discussed poverty, schools, child care, the solutions, and the prospects. I allowed as how I simply could not support the Bush budget without mandatory funding for IDEA. Dodd was convinced it would never happen and suggested that I should announce my opposition to the budget. I wasn't ready for that, but I wondered aloud whether there was room for me in the Republican Party anymore. Chris moved to the edge of his seat, almost rising. He quickly assured me that there was always room for me in the Democratic Party, and that they'd love to have me. I told him I could never be a Democrat, but that I could be an Independent. Neither of us knew whether to take the discussion seriously, and we left it by joking about the commotion such a decision would cause.

On the walk back to my office in the Hart Building, Ken Connolly asked me if I had really been thinking seriously about leaving the Republican Party. I smiled at him and dismissed it, but it wouldn't be too long before we spoke of it again.

As long as I had been in the Senate my Democratic colleagues had kidded me about switching parties. And when Senator Richard Shelby of Alabama switched from the Democratic to Republican Party in 1994, one of my conservative detractors suggested that he be swapped for me so the Republicans could be rid of me. But these had been good-natured, or at least whimsical, suggestions. Not until it came out of my mouth in Chris Dodd's office that Friday had I spoken aloud what had been on my mind.

Nothing came of our conversation for a while, but I am sure that Chris, directly or indirectly, passed our conversation along to the Democratic Leader, Tom Daschle of South Dakota. Probably not by coincidence, a month after my meeting with Senator Dodd, Senator Bill Nelson of Florida, with whom I had served in the House, called to ask me to meet with him. On the morning of April 30, we met and he talked at some length about the party switch of Senator Shelby years before. I mostly listened.

The night of Monday, May 14, Tom Daschle asked me to meet with him and Harry Reid of Nevada, the Democratic Whip, the following morning. Tom and I had followed similar paths to the Senate, by first winning our small states' at-large seats in the U.S. House of Representatives, where we had worked closely together on Vietnam veterans issues. I talked about my increasing discomfort in the Republican Party. They talked about how eager they were to have me join their ranks, at least for organizational purposes.

No surprise there. In a Senate split right down the middle, the defection of one member would make an enormous difference. Daschle and Reid would have been guilty of political malpractice if they hadn't been talking to me and anybody else they thought they could approach, just as Trent would have been foolish not to have been working on Zell Miller or Ben Nelson or any other Democratic prospect.

Had Lott succeeded in persuading a Democrat to switch, Republicans would have hailed him as a genius. Indeed, the defections of Senators Shelby and Ben Nighthorse Campbell of Colorado in 1994 and 1995 had been greeted in Republican circles as statesmanlike decisions that affirmed the righteousness of all that was Republican. When Long Island House member Michael Forbes switched to the Democratic Party in 1999, by contrast, Republicans regarded him as having joined the undead, and they put a stake through his heart in the election a year later.

As I walked back to my office after the meeting with Daschle and Reid, I was reasonably certain that I should leave the Republican Party. I was about to have that confidence shaken.

As soon as I arrived at my office in the Hart Building, I went to see Susan Russ. I was not really sure how she would respond, but I had no doubt she would be surprised. In the past, whenever this subject came up, no matter how casually, Susan would always cover her ears and say she didn't even want to talk about it. I am not sure what was different this time, but when I entered her office and told her I had just met with Daschle and Reid, she put her head in her hands and said, "Let's talk."

We talked for over an hour. She ran through some of the more obvious reasons I should reconsider and a few that had not been so obvious. It was clear to her, without even asking, that I had already determined this was something I should do, and she did not feel any need to give me encouragement in that direction. Susan went through the impact this would have on staff and on my career and relationships in the Senate, and the fallout from and for Vermont.

I explained that I had told Daschle and Reid that I believed this was something I should do, that I would become an Independent and vote with the Democrats for organizational purposes. I had also told them that I wanted to do this with the least negative impact on my state and my staff.

I had been assured that my seniority would be honored and they would do what they could to accommodate staff who were displaced. While this was the best I could hope for, for several of the Republicans on my committee staff it would be small comfort. As one conservative member of my staff later joked, "If they say they are going to take care of me, I'll be waiting for the Sopranos to show up at my doorstep." Harry Reid also had very generously told me that he would be willing to step down as chairman of the Environment and Public Works Committee so that I would retain a chairmanship. This would, of course, be subject to approval by the Democratic caucus.

Susan was trying to track down Mark Powden, and at this point asked Ken Connolly to join us. Ken was initially shocked, though his reaction was more mixed given his interest in environmental issues and the possibility of my becoming chairman of the environment committee.

Susan was still trying to find Mark. As the staff director of the Health, Education, Labor, and Pensions Committee, it would be his staff who would suffer the most direct consequences when this happened. He is also one of my closest advisers and I wanted to have him in on the discussion.

It was now approaching noon and Bill Kurtz, my former campaign manager and my new state director, arrived from Vermont. His trip had been planned for some time, but the timing now seemed quite fortuitous. Bill, like the others, was surprised and clearly concerned, but he kept his own counsel. We quickly caught him up on what we had been discussing and what I had in mind. Soon after, Mark arrived.

Mark's reaction was typically somewhat more subdued than Susan's, but he too was clearly concerned. I left for lunch around one and can only imagine the conversation that ensued among the staff I left behind. When I returned about two hours later, they were still meeting. Susan's list of concerns had grown as Bill was focused on the logistics of where, when, and how such a decision would become public.

I remember clearly two things that came up at that brief meeting. Bill reminded me that I would be giving up the longest continually held Republican seat in history, and Susan had a list of my closest colleagues and what my move would cost them. My anxiety was beginning to return.

My wife Liz arrived later that afternoon to work on a project for the Senate spouses, at this point unaware of the discussion. Although I had talked to her at some length about my frustrations and had occasionally vented that I should leave the party, we had not discussed this as a real possibility. I had wanted to talk to Liz privately about this the night before my meeting with Daschle and Reid, but she had a class that night and I had been traveling all weekend and Monday. I was tired.

I was also probably just avoiding the confrontation I anticipated.

When Liz walked into Susan's office, it did not take her a nanosecond to see that something big was happening. She asked what was going on, and as I searched for just the right words, Susan rather bluntly informed her that "Jim just told us that he is seriously considering switching parties." I quickly corrected her and said I would leave the Republican Party and become an Independent. I am not sure why I thought the distinction might lessen the impact.

Liz expressed her concerns while acknowledging that she knew how frustrated and miserable I had been. Her concerns were more of a personal nature than those expressed by staff. She had become very close to many of the Senate wives, particularly Republican spouses, and was keenly aware of what hurt this would cause them and their families. She also was very concerned about our son Leonard and his wife Maura who have more conservative political beliefs and would definitely be upset by such a move on my part.

Leonard and Maura and my daughter Laura have lived nearby in Washington over the years. Laura is less conservative than her brother, and I thought she would be more comfortable with whatever decision I made. But from our lively debates around the kitchen table, I knew that would not be the case with Len and Maura.

As I listened to the arguments that afternoon, I looked around at Liz and the staff and felt a profound sadness but a growing sense that what I planned to do was right. I was not sure it was right personally, but I was very confident it was the right thing to do for the country. Over the next ten days, I would revisit that decision several times.

SOMEBODY WAS leaking my meetings with the Democrats to the press. Almost as soon as I got back to the office, Erik Smulson got a call from CNN asking about a possible party change. Later in the day, Peter Freyne, a columnist for *Seven Days,* an alternative weekly in Vermont, asked the same question. Erik was ready to make the same flat denial he had made for years, but Susan reeled him in so he wouldn't be put in the position of lying to the press. Instead, he put out a statement that should have served as a neon sign.

On Wednesday, May 16, Freyne's column came out quoting Erik as saying that "Senator Jeffords is comfortable as the most conservative member of the Vermont delegation, and regardless of party label, will do what he thinks is right for Vermont and the nation." As Freyne aptly concluded, "That didn't sound like an absolute 'no,' did it?"

Thursday was strangely quiet. My conversations with staff continued, but to my surprise no one had picked up the Freyne column. I called former Vermont Senator Bob Stafford, the one person outside of my immediate circle with whom I would discuss my possible switch. Bob had preceded me in the Senate and had chaired the Senate Education Subcommittee, as I would a few years later. He was instrumental in strengthening federal education efforts and had sat across from me in many conferences between the House and Senate on education, beginning with IDEA in 1975. My family felt especially close to Bob. When he was young our house was on his newspaper route, and he used our lawn for sledding, as he described it, not necessarily with my father's permission.

Before entering Congress, Bob had served several terms as Vermont's Governor and Attorney General. In the latter capacity he represented the State of Vermont before the Vermont Supreme Court, on which, for a time, my father served as Chief Justice. Bob is a great storyteller, usually at his own expense, and recounts how one day he was arguing before my father and the other justices and was making absolutely no headway. Rather than pushing his line of reasoning any further, he concluded by observing that "Your Honor, I can see that I am just beating my head against a wall." To which my father replied, "Mr. Attorney General, I assure you that no one could do so with less fear of personal injury."

When I reached him by phone, Bob was his usual warm, gracious, and thoughtful self. He had tangled with the Republican Party enough during his own career to know something of what I was going through, but he had always remained loyal to it. While he didn't necessarily agree with my switching, neither did he presume that the political environment of the Senate today is the same as the one that he left thirteen years ago.

Our hometown paper, *The Rutland Herald*, picked up the story on Friday, and its article was excerpted in *The Hotline*, a daily political tip sheet. Although *The Hotline* buried it, CNN's Jonathan Karl called the office to follow up on it. Erik directed him to the online version of the Rutland paper, and by the end of the day Karl was stirring the pot of speculation:

Democrats are reaching out very aggressively to Jeffords, trying to get him to switch parties, come over to the Democratic Party. He is now openly flirting with the idea of possibly switching parties. One thing under consideration in these talks between Jeffords and the Democrats would be potentially for Jeffords to become an independent but to vote for Tom Daschle and the Democratic leadership.

Once this report went on the air, Karl's phone immediately began to ring, with calls from the Lott office, the Daschle office, and the White House. Despite its call, the White House later claimed it had no sense that I might leave the party until the early part of the following week. Daschle was reportedly greatly concerned by Friday's report because he was certain it would prompt an immediate response from the White House.*

Throughout the day I had been meeting with Susan, Mark, and Bill to discuss whether and how I should leave the party. We kicked around ideas as to how to unveil the decision if I went ahead with it, and whether it would make more sense to do so before or after the week-long recess that would begin on Friday, May 25. We talked about how such a decision would affect the major issues then before the Senate. While the education bill would be relatively unaffected given the broad consensus be-

* *Washington Post* reporter Howard Kurtz first noted the discrepancy in the White House comments in his story of May 27, 2001.

hind it, early on I determined to avoid tipping the balance on the tax bill. We all decided the best thing to do was to think more about this; perhaps I would wait until after the Memorial Day recess to make a final decision. Liz and I were planning to go on a trip to Italy to an environmental conference sponsored by the nonpartisan Aspen Institute that week. Everyone around me thought I should take time to reflect; however, I think everyone knew at some level that my decision was made.

Throughout the week, the staff was very concerned that if I was going to make a switch, that it be done on my terms and not just leaked out in dribbles. I suspect a few still harbored the hope that I would change my mind before this became public.

Over the weekend, ABC News reported that I was "seriously toying with switching parties." Asked about the possibility on a Sunday-morning television talk show, Lott denied it would happen, remarking in jest that it would mean the end of the Singing Senators.

Watching Trent on television in the living room with Liz, I knew better. In fact, the Singing Senators had probably died in December when I cast a vote for Pete Domenici in a Republican leadership race against fellow Singing Senator and Lott ally Larry Craig.

Since I considered Larry a friend, I departed from the

usual custom and had given him an honest answer when he came to my office and asked me for my vote. Usually, both candidates in these secret ballot elections enter them with commitments from a majority of the caucus. But I thought Pete would provide a more moderate voice, and I told Larry so. Although John Ashcroft's nomination for attorney general would have meant the end of our little group sooner or later, I was not invited to sing with the Singing Senators again.

Sunday evening, Liz and I went into my office to catch up on some correspondence. I was surprised to see Susan there, as working Sundays is not her usual style. However, it was clear these were unusual times. Susan told me that she really needed to talk with me one on one without mincing words. We had a quiet but very intense conversation. At the end, I told her that I believed she had made many good points and that I would continue to keep an open mind, not making any firm commitment until after the recess. I meant that, but I was also becoming more and more convinced that even if I waited a week or two weeks, my decision would be the same. Susan told me that if I did decide to switch, she would support me.

By May 21, the next day, even though I had told both Liz and Susan that I would wait until after the recess, I knew it could not wait. Liz informed Susan early Monday morning that it was clear to her that my decision was made and we should all just go about doing what we needed to do. I confirmed that by midday.

That morning, the conservative *Washington Times*, often the best source for Republican thinking, reported:

> Top Republicans told The Times that the best evidence that Mr. Jeffords is not, at the moment, about to leave the party is that the Bush White House is not on the phone to Mr. Jeffords or his friends trying to dissuade him from doing so.
>
> "Believe me, the Bush White House political operation would be all over Vermont trying to stop that if it were about to happen," a Republican close to the White House said.

Seeing the growing news coverage, my son Leonard called me at the office on Monday to ask me my plans. I told him I had not fully made up my mind, but that I was leaning toward becoming an Independent. He gave me some arguments against such a switch, and we left it at that. The next day, his wife Maura came by the office to deliver a trivet emblazoned with an elephant and a letter in which they made the tongue-in-cheek vow to name their first-born child "Reagan Nixon Jeffords" as my replacement if I left the Republican Party.

My fellow moderate Republican, Olympia Snowe of Maine, was concerned enough by the question posed to Lott on Sunday that she sought me out on Monday night on the Senate floor. When I told her I was seriously thinking of switching, she was surprised and upset, as I had not shared anything like this at the weekly Wednesday lunch of the small band of Republican moderates from the Northeast.

Soon after we finished, Olympia called a fellow New Englander, Bush's Chief of Staff Andy Card, to let him know I was seriously considering switching. But he had left the White House for the day and they did not connect until the following morning.

By Tuesday, May 22, the Republican leadership and seemingly the entire Senate was fully aware of my thinking. As we cast vote after vote throughout the day, Senators stopped by my desk to make conversation. Don Nickles admonished me to stop drinking whatever funny water I had found. Trent Lott and Larry Craig talked about reviving the Singing Senators. Democrat Jay Rockefeller of West Virginia went away beaming when I told him of my intentions. Republican Phil Gramm of Texas, who had switched from the Democratic Party to the

Republican while a House member in the 1980s, allowed that he might do the same thing if he had my political views. "Just don't screw up the tax bill," he volunteered.

In the midst of the visits and the votes, I met off the Senate floor with Trent Lott at ten and Vice President Cheney at noon, and in the Oval Office with the President at two. I told each of them I was strongly considering leaving the party, and I tried my best to describe my thinking.

By the time I met with the President on Tuesday afternoon he was briefed on my earlier meetings and must have known that he faced a nearly impossible task in dissuading me. He was relaxed and charming, and did his best to impress upon me the consequences of handing control of the Senate to the Democrats. I tried to use my time to convince him of the need to govern more from the center. Coming from me, I doubt it was very convincing. But I argued that like his father he would be a one-term President if he didn't go beyond the conservative Republican base on such issues as providing greater resources for education.

I also volunteered that if I decided to leave the party, I would do so in a way that would not jeopardize the tax bill. It may have been a small thing, but it struck me as a fair way to balance my actions against his and Republican interests generally, and he thanked me for it.

While I had worked well with the White House on some issues, I didn't relish the continuing role of a spoiler, someone regarded as more of a nuisance than an ally. I suppose that I had heard what I wanted to hear from candidate Bush, thinking he would govern more as a uniter, not a divider, and that the compassion would trump the conservative. At least on the budget and tax bills, that had not been the case.

And while I had regarded Trent as a friend, his actions made me doubt our friendship. His lack of candor on petty things made me question whether I could trust him on anything of importance. That doubt has since been largely removed.

I called my daughter Laura at her office in an architectural firm in downtown Washington. I told her that I planned to announce that I was leaving the Republican Party the following day.

Laura shares my idealism and optimism, and would send me off for work every morning with the exhortation to "Save the world, Jim." And every day I have tried to live up to her rather lofty expectations. Liz and I have taught our children not to give up. But I think Laura wondered whether I had.

Her immediate reaction to my call was one of stomach-wrenching fear at the consequences. She asked me if I was okay; if the staff, particularly Susan and Mark, were okay; and finally, what the fallout would be.

I could give her a decent answer to the first two questions, but didn't really have an answer for the third. She knew I would be labeled a traitor by Republicans and worried for me. After we spoke for a minute or so, she asked, "You're not running again, are you?" It wasn't really a question, and I didn't answer. I doubted it, but it was the furthest thing from my thoughts at that point.

Like everyone close to me, Laura wanted to be sure I had really thought through my decision. When it was clear to her that I had, she gave me her full support. She understood this was the biggest moment of my career and didn't try to convince me otherwise. She knew firsthand the sacrifices I had made over the course of my career, was sad I had reached this point, but was certain I had made the right decision.

Just after the Cheney meeting at noon and before the Bush meeting at two, I sat down with my staff in my office in the Capitol and instructed them on what I wanted in the speech I planned to give the next day. While I would have liked to deliver the speech at home in Vermont, at the time I assumed I would either deliver it on the floor of the Senate or via a conference call with the Vermont press corps. We were still in the midst of votes on the tax bill, and I thought it would be derelict to leave before we had finished our work.

I had shared most of my thinking with Susan and Mark during the past week of discussions as they had played devil's advocate and then some. It was the first time we had all focused together on the reasons to make the switch without discussing the other side of the ledger.

Mark pulled out a yellow pad and said, "Okay, Jim, why do you want to do this?" I went through my reasoning yet again, answering the questions they posed. Mark took notes. When I finished, it was clear to me that even though they had initially disagreed with the decision, they understood.

The next morning, the media siege began in earnest, with camera crews parked outside the house when we awoke. Walking to work was out of the question. Liz jested that we moon them to give them something for their trouble, but I thought a smile and a wave would suffice.

I went from my house straight to the Capitol, but the business on the Senate floor would consume little of my time or attention that Wednesday, May 23. At ten, at the request of John Warner, I joined about ten mostly moderate Republicans in the Vice President's Room to discuss what I was thinking of doing later that day. Almost everyone talked about their committees, their chairs, and their agendas. They asked me to reconsider and proposed finding yet another configuration of power sharing between the two parties to supplant the one so painfully negotiated between Lott and Daschle at the beginning of the Congress. At the end of the meeting, Linc Chafee chimed in and said that in spite of what I was hearing, I had to go forward with what I felt in my heart. I had to stick to my principles. I could have hugged him.

Given the difficulty of reaching the first agreement on power sharing in the evenly divided Senate at the outset of the Congress, I didn't see much prospect for a second. They also asked that I delay any announcement for a day, and I felt I owed them that much. This meeting, like every meeting, gave rise to rumors and a rash of calls to me and my staff. Daschle heard from Warner that there would be a new proposal on power sharing, a prospect he must have dreaded. But all I had agreed to was to think about it and to meet again later that afternoon.

At midday, I sat down to go over the speech drafted the day before. Generally it captured what I wanted to say, but I thought it could be strengthened by giving the audience a better understanding of how independence is a treasured trait of Vermonters.

One of our early Representatives in the U.S. House, Matthew Lyon, was a fierce Jeffersonian Republican. When he continued to print anti-Federalist articles in his newspaper he became the first Member of Congress convicted of a felony, tried and found guilty of violating the Sedition Act. The Vermont electorate responded by re-electing him to Congress from the Vergennes, Vermont jail. And since he could not or would not put up bail money, there he sat as the 1800 presidential election was heading to the House of Representatives to be decided.

Finally bailed out by a Virginia ally of Jefferson's, he returned to Washington to cast one of the critical votes that gave Jefferson the presidency. He was a man of the frontier. He soon left Vermont for Kentucky, which he also represented in the House only to move yet again to the Arkansas Territory, a far cry from his native Ireland.

As Vermont was the bane of the Federalists, by the middle of the century it had become perhaps the greatest irritant in the country to the Democrats and the South in their efforts to expand the reach of slavery into the territories. Vermonters sent petition after petition to Congress and made almost no effort to return runaway slaves.

Its representatives in Congress were among the most vocal in their calls for an end to slavery, which had been outlawed in the Republic of Vermont's Constitution of 1777.

Vermonters were strongly opposed to the admission of Texas to the Union so long as it did not renounce slavery. In 1844, the Vermont legislature voted 120 to 48 to oppose the annexation as "unconstitutional, inexpedient, and unjust."

The stream of antislavery petitions from Vermont went unabated. While it has not been documented with certainty, the story goes that the Georgia House resolved that its governor "be and is hereby requested to transmit the Vermont resolutions to the deep, dank, and fetid sink of social and political iniquity from whence they emanated, with the following unequivocal declaration inscribed thereon: Resolved, That Georgia standing on her constitutional palladium, heeds not the maniac ravings of hellborn fanaticism, nor stoops from her lofty position to hold terms with perjured traitors."

The Georgia Senate reportedly responded by requesting President Franklin Pierce "to employ a sufficient number of able-bodied Irishmen to proceed to the State of Vermont, and to dig a ditch around the limits of the same, and to float 'the thing' into the Atlantic."

Pierce, a native of New Hampshire, which stands between Vermont and the Atlantic, is not known to have responded.

For the century following the Civil War, Vermont was the mirror image of the solidly Democratic South. Like the South, elections were decided in the primary—in our case, the Republican one. Even in the depths of the Depression and in the midst of the Roosevelt landslide of 1936, Vermont remained true to the Republican Party and Alf Landon, one of only two states to do so.

The other, Maine, had been such a reliable bellwether of national elections to that point that the expression "As Maine goes, so goes the Nation" was coined. In the wake of 1936, it was amended to "As Maine goes, so goes Vermont."

But while the rest of the country may have thought Vermont's views were out of step, Vermonters had no doubts. A Burlington newspaper headline trumpeted "Vermont Stands Firm While Rest of Nation Follows Strange Gods."

While no follower of Roosevelt, our governor and later senator, George Aiken, was pleading with his party to adopt a more compassionate approach to the millions of people out of work with only a patchwork support system to fall back upon. Aiken went on to become the chairman of the Senate Agriculture Committee and a critical advocate for our nation's nutrition programs.

Vermont has never suffered tyrants, foreign or domestic. The State declared war on the Nazis six months before Pearl Harbor. After the war, Aiken was joined in the Senate by Ralph Flanders, a Senator who had begun his career as a teenage apprentice in the machine tool industry. Flanders led the efforts to censure Senator Joseph McCarthy. I can close my eyes and still see him handing the note to McCarthy informing him that he would take to the Senate floor later that day to denounce his conduct. Flanders was a remarkable man, and not just for his political courage. He was an inventor credited with important developments in the machine tool industry, and a largely self-educated author on everything from developments in his industry to sociology.

The political heir of Aiken and Flanders was my friend Bob Stafford. In the 1980s, Bob and five other moderate Republican Senators formed the "Gang of Six," six Republican Senators who often clashed with the Reagan Administration over issues such as education and the environment. They, along with those of us who formed the Republican "Gypsy Moth" group in the House, did our best to ensure that critical functions of government were not undercut.

All of this was far too much to cram into one short speech, but I hoped to give listeners a sense of Vermont's history, and what I considered to be my history. I was under no illusion about how much people across the nation knew about me. It was absolutely nothing.

In fact, not too long ago this was brought home with dead-on accuracy. I went through Yale on a Navy ROTC scholarship, and after graduation I was commissioned as an officer on the U.S.S. *McNair,* a destroyer that would be the first U.S. ship up the Suez Canal when it reopened in 1956. Every few years the officers from my days aboard gather for a reunion near Norfolk, Virginia. In 1993, the newsletter prior to the reunion read as follows:

> We had thought that on the occasion of such an important reunion we might be able to have the President of the United States address us at dinner on Saturday. It looks now, however, that the best we will probably be able to do is have an obscure Senator from a small state.

GOOD FRIENDS will keep you humble. But by Wednesday, May 23, the obscurity was starting to wear off. We were casting one vote after another, and every news outlet was running the story almost nonstop. Camera crews had staked out my office in the Senate Hart Building, so to avoid them I spent most of the day in my office in the Capitol, trying to travel as many different routes as possible to elude the press. It didn't take long for the dozens of photographers and reporters covering the story to figure out my route from the office to the floor for votes. By the afternoon, the stairway to my Capitol office became packed with press, and the basement corridor between the office and the Senate floor, usually home for no one but off-duty tour guides and Capitol police, had become a gauntlet of flashing cameras. This only added to the fatigue felt by me and everyone else.

The last thing I needed to do before leaving for Vermont at eight that night was to meet once more with my Republican colleagues in the Vice President's Room. This meeting was by far the toughest, and my staff argued it was pointless to put everyone through it since it would likely only rehash the arguments from the morning.

But I felt I owed my colleagues at least this much— one more chance to hear from me why I was planning to switch, and one more chance, however remote, to talk me out of it.

I got to the meeting late, and found the group from the morning meeting had reassembled along with a few new faces. I don't remember the exact order of speakers, it was something of a blur. But I remember one of my colleagues, a chairman who would soon have to hand over his gavel to the Democrats, who had barely begun his remarks when he broke down. I soon had tears in my eyes as well, overcome with emotion, and barely able to speak. I was offered a non-elected position in the Republican leadership to serve as a voice for the moderates, and help on the causes near and dear to me.

Outside the room much of the Senate awaited. I'm sure Senator Daschle was anxious, having thought he might be Majority Leader by now but instead facing further delay. My staff, which had been scrambling through the day to make arrangements to get me back to Vermont and book the biggest room they could find in the state, wondered what this last meeting might produce as the minutes passed by and the time when I would need to head home neared.

While we were talking, so was my staff. Ken spoke with my scheduler, Trecia McEvoy, to find out when I needed to get back to the house to pack for Vermont. He came in to our meeting and whispered in my ear that it was time to go. I suspected, as did probably all the Senators, that he was also giving me an excuse to leave if I was looking for one. John Warner, sitting on the edge of the Vice President's desk, asked for another minute.

Ken left the room, but five minutes later returned. I really did need to get going, and there was nothing more to be said. I rose to leave, John asked me to remain, but it was time to go. As I walked down the lobby that runs behind the Senate, Senator Ted Stevens of Alaska caught up with me. A man of character, he assured me that regardless of my decision our friendship would remain intact. It meant a lot to me, but I was too overcome with emotion to respond with more than a few words.

HAVING MADE my final decision on the flight up to Burlington, I arrived tired but at peace. The other passengers left the plane as Liz, Erik, Susan, and I waited. When a few minutes later we walked into the terminal, even the media circus in Washington had not prepared us for what we encountered. We could see a mass of people and cameras in the main part of the airport and knew we could not get through the crowd unassisted.

Erik went ahead to find the two members of my Vermont staff who were to meet us, Jeff Munger and Bill Kurtz. When they returned, Erik told me that he had never seen such a crowd of press in Vermont and we would just have to keep our heads low and plow through. We proceeded through the airport, seeing some familiar faces from the Vermont press corps and an awful lot of folks we did not know. We also heard the cheers from beyond the cameras and saw numerous signs, both positive and negative.

When we arrived at the Sheraton Hotel, a little after ten, we needed to edit the speech to incorporate some changes I had made. Erik had a laptop but no printer. When we called the front desk to see about using their business center, we found out it was closed. I really wanted to have a final speech text to work on that night if I could not sleep, and certainly early the next morning at the latest.

As we discussed options, the staff at the front desk called to say that they would open the office for as long as I needed and do anything else they could to help. We made the changes on the laptop, Erik went down to print it out, and Liz and I watched the late night news. At midnight, Erik slipped the finished speech under my door. I read it once and promptly fell asleep.

I slept soundly for the first time in weeks. I rose early and reviewed the speech several times before I had breakfast with Liz. At nine sharp, Jeff and Susan arrived to pick us up. Although it does not take thirty minutes to drive from the Sheraton to the Radisson where the press conference was to take place, I am notoriously late for everything. A fifteen-minute padding is standard to account for this, but this morning, I was ready to go.

As we drove to the hotel, Susan joked that it was not too late to change my mind if I wanted to. I assured her I would not be doing that. Liz reminded me that I needed to slow down when I spoke, not to race through the speech. Erik called at 9:25 A.M. and told us to head on to the hotel. He alerted us that there were a lot of people in front of the Radisson Hotel but that police had been called and we would have an escort into the press conference room.

I could scarcely believe the sight that awaited me as we turned the corner. A dozen satellite trucks were parked on the street that ran between the hotel and the long blue expanse of Lake Champlain.

Hundreds of people had gathered. At the front of their ranks stood a costumed Benedict Arnold, making me believe for an instant that the entire crowd had come to protest my decision. But as we drew closer, I could see the signs of supporters outnumbered the few in opposition. I thanked Liz for her constant pressure to focus on the speech rather than leaving it to the last minute, as is my usual custom.

And once I got out of the car there was no mistaking

the positive energy of the crowd. The Burlington police had their hands full keeping the people back so we could make our way into the hotel and through the lobby. As we did, I was incredibly touched by all the familiar faces of friends and former staff who had made the effort to be with me, and I was buoyed by the cheers of the crowd.

Throughout the day, perfect strangers were extraordinarily helpful with all our last-minute requests and needs, from the police to the staff of the Sheraton where I had spent the night to the staff of the Radisson where I spoke. It had almost happened by accident, but I was tremendously grateful I had come home, to Vermont.

Even though we had been forced by the sheer num-|bers to allow only reporters into the banquet room of the hotel, it was mobbed with press from around the world. Seven months earlier, when I had delivered my speech to the Burlington Rotary a few blocks away in the final weeks of the campaign, perhaps two reporters attended.

But just outside the room, the hotel lobby was jammed with hundreds of people who had come for the event. And as I began my speech, I could hear their applause and shouts of support. Not expecting members of the public to be at the press conference, I had not anticipated any vocal response to my words. Awkwardly, I found myself apologizing to the press in the middle of my remarks for the interruption. But it sure felt good.

I found my rhythm. Thanks to Liz, the words were by now familiar, and more important, they were from the heart. I believed then that I was absolutely doing the right thing for the country, my state, and myself. It was not without costs to me and to others, but I was certain I had made the right decision. As I concluded and left the hall, I was nearly carried out of the hotel by the enthusiastic response of the Vermonters in attendance.

III

FIVE

My Declaration

Burlington, Vermont
May 24, 2001

Anyone who knows me, knows I love the State of Vermont.

It has always been known for its independence and social conscience. It was the first state to outlaw slavery in its constitution. It proudly elected Matthew Lyon to Congress, despite his flouting of the Sedition Act. It sacrificed a higher share of its sons to the Civil War than perhaps any other state in the Union.

I recall Vermont Senator Ralph Flanders' dramatic statement almost fifty years ago, helping to bring to a close the McCarthy hearings, a sorry chapter in our history.

Today's chapter is of much smaller consequence, but I think it appropriate that I share my thoughts with my fellow Vermonters.

For the past several weeks, I have been struggling with a very difficult decision. It is difficult on a personal level, but it is even more difficult because of its larger impact on the Senate and the nation.

I've been talking with my family and a few close advisers about whether or not I should remain a Republican. I do not approach this question lightly. I have spent a lifetime in the Republican Party, and served for twelve years in what I believe is the longest continuously held Republican seat in the U.S. Senate. I ran for reelection as a Republican just last fall, and had no thoughts whatsoever then about changing parties.

The party I grew up in was the party of George Aiken, Ernest Gibson, Ralph Flanders, and Bob Stafford. These names may not mean much today outside Vermont. But each served Vermont as a Republican Senator in the twentieth century.

I became a Republican not because I was born into the party but because of the kind of fundamental principles that these and many other Republicans stood for— moderation, tolerance, and fiscal responsibility. Their party—our party—was the party of Lincoln.

To be sure, we had our differences in the Vermont Republican Party. But even our more conservative leaders were in many ways progressive. Our former governor, Deane Davis, championed Act 250, which preserved our environmental heritage. And Vermont's Calvin Coolidge, our nation's thirtieth president, could point with pride to our state's willingness to sacrifice in the service of others.

Aiken and Gibson and Flanders and Stafford were all Republicans. But they were Vermonters first. They spoke their minds, often to the dismay of their party leaders, and did their best to guide the party in the direction of our fundamental principles.

For twenty-six years in Washington, first in the House of Representatives and now in the Senate, I have tried to do the same. But I can no longer do so.

Increasingly, I find myself in disagreement with my party. I understand that many people are more conservative than I am, and they form the Republican Party. Given the changing nature of the national party, it has become a struggle for our leaders to deal with me, and for me to deal with them.

Indeed, the party's electoral success has underscored the dilemma I face within my party.

In the past, without the presidency, the various wings of the Republican Party in Congress have had some freedom to argue and ultimately to shape the party's agenda. The election of President Bush changed that dramatically. We don't live in a parliamentary system, but it is only natural to expect that people such as myself, who have been honored with positions of leadership, will largely support the president's agenda.

And yet more and more, I find I cannot. Those who don't know me may have thought I took pleasure in resisting the President's budget, or that I enjoyed the limelight. Nothing could be further from the truth. I had serious, substantive reservations about that budget, and the decisions it sets in place for today and the future.

Looking ahead, I can see more and more instances where I will disagree with the President on very fundamental issues: the issues of choice, the direction of the judiciary, tax and spending decisions, missile defense, energy and the environment, and a host of other issues, large and small.

The largest for me is education. I come from the state of Justin Smith Morrill, a U.S. Senator who gave America the land grant college system. His Republican Party stood for opportunity for all, for opening the doors of public school education to every American child. Now, for some, success seems to be measured by the number of students moved out of public schools.

In order to best represent my state of Vermont, my own conscience, and the principles I have stood for my whole life, I will leave the Republican Party and become an Independent. Control of the Senate will soon be changed by my decision. I will make this change and will caucus with the Democrats for organizational purposes, once the conference report on the tax bill is sent to the President.

My colleagues, many of them my friends for years, may find it difficult in their hearts to befriend me any longer. Many of my supporters will be disappointed, and some of my staffers will see their lives upended. I regret this very much. Having made my decision, the weight that has been lifted from my shoulders now hangs on my heart.

But I was not elected to this office to be something that I am not. This comes as no surprise to Vermonters, because independence is the Vermont way. My friends back home have supported and encouraged my independence even when they did not agree with my decisions. I appreciate the support they have shown when they have agreed with me, and their patience when they have not. I will ask for that support and patience again, which I understand will be difficult for a number of my friends.

I have informed President Bush, Vice President Cheney, and Senator Lott of my decision. They are good people with whom I disagree. They have been fair and decent to me. I have also informed Senator Daschle of my decision. Three of these four men disagreed with my decision, but I hope each understood my reasons. And it is entirely possible that the fourth may well have second thoughts down the road.

I have changed my party label, but I have not changed my beliefs. Indeed, my decision is about affirming the principles that have shaped my career. I hope the people of Vermont will understand it. I hope in time that my colleagues will as well. I am confident that it is the right decision.

WHEN WE pulled away from the Radisson, Liz told me I had done a great job and that she was proud of me. Liz is the most honest person I know—in fact, painfully so at times—and her compliment meant the world to me. Susan, sitting in the back seat with Liz, admitted that she could not bring herself to be in the room at the time of the speech, pacing outside the press conference instead and watching the amazing crowd that had formed there. Jeff Munger, who was driving, concurred with Liz and said it was the best speech he had ever heard me deliver.

About two minutes later, Tom Daschle called to congratulate and compliment me on my speech. It looked like my twenty-six-year plan to lower expectations of my speaking ability had finally paid off.

The next call came from Darcie Johnston, whom I have known since she was born. Her dad, Jimmy, is my good friend and first campaign manager. Darcie had been working on my campaigns since she was old enough to hand out a flyer and stuff an envelope. She had since worked on my congressional staff and now had her own fund-raising business, which I used during my last campaign. Darcie is a rock-solid Republican and had been very active in all of the Bush for President campaigns. Days before, she had expressed her sincere hope that I would not make the switch, but now she was calling in tears to say she still wished I had decided differently but she would support me personally.

We arrived back at the Sheraton and went to our room. Bill Kurtz arrived shortly and I began to get phone calls. Senator Edward Kennedy of Massachusetts called, as did Vermont Democratic Governor Howard Dean. Ted and Howard are friends of mine as well as colleagues, and their calls in support were much appreciated. Pat Leahy also called. Pat had been aware of the turmoil of the past week and had offered quiet support behind the scenes. I greatly valued that support, as I know the press had been hounding him all week.

Soon after we arrived back at the Sheraton, I had an opportunity to meet with most of my Vermont staff who had traveled from my three offices around the state. They had come to help where they could and to provide encouragement. Like their colleagues in Washington, not all of them would have made the same decision, but once it was made, they have been tremendous in their support. Right after this meeting, Liz left to catch an earlier plane back to D.C. With our daughter-in-law's graduation from law school that weekend, we were having a lot of company and she was anxious to get back home and get things in order. Erik had returned from the Radisson and was reviewing some of the questions that were likely to come up in the press conference later that day.

Having come home to Vermont to make my announcement, I needed to spend some time with the Vermont press. The past month had been so hectic, I had been available far less than customary. I certainly had not discussed my pending decision, and I knew they were beginning to get a little irritated. It was only fair to give them a chance to talk with me about my decision. Although I felt my speech could speak for itself, I also wanted to be sure Vermonters had a full explanation.

While I was meeting with the Vermont reporters, we received several calls letting us know that death threats were beginning to come in from a variety of quarters. Apparently the phone lines in my offices were so jammed that some individuals who wanted to make death threats were unable to get through. Being more eager than clever, a few callers began dialing seemingly any Vermont phone number, including those of the Vermont state police barracks and the Vermont State House. This was brought to Governor Dean's attention. He immediately dispatched a member of the Vermont state police to come to the Sheraton and arranged for the police to begin assessing the veracity of these threats.

Lord knows I had spent much of the past ten days talking about the kinds of reactions that would attend a decision to leave the party. However, threats on my life had never come up. This type of thing has become all too commonplace. But it is still so discordant with our democracy that the idea had never even crossed my mind.

Soon after, both an officer from the Vermont state police and an agent from the FBI were assigned to protect me. I did not know it at the time, but this was just the beginning of three weeks of around-the-clock security. Although for the most part I felt I was safe and knew that most of the threats were harmless venting, it was unsettling for me, my family, and my staff to know that there were people who might really try something.

After the press conference, I decided to go back to my room in the hotel and rest a few hours until my flight back to Washington. My staff decided to go down to the Sheraton lounge to watch the news and perhaps have a drink. After about an hour, I realized I could not sleep. With my new security entourage accompanying me, I went to join Erik, Bill, and Susan.

Earlier that morning, as had been planned months before my decision, I had addressed the annual Vermont Business Expo under way at the hotel by videotape. Immediately following my taped address, almost the entire crowd at the expo watched my live speech on a television screen that had been brought into the hall.

Many of the Vermont businessmen and -women attending the convention were now gathering in the lounge. When I entered it, their heartfelt expressions of support were overwhelming. I made my way to the table where my staff sat and joined them as we watched the early edition of the local news. My announcement was the lead story. There was the usual buzz of conversation in the room until a reporter on the television interviewed a man who expressed the opinion that someone should shoot me for what I had done.

The room went silent. It is one thing to learn you are

receiving anonymous death threats; it is quite another to watch and hear those words from a fellow human being.

After a few seconds when it soaked in, our conversation returned to more prosaic matters—the logistics of getting to the airport. We went on about our business, but it seemed as though we all felt a sudden weariness. The day was catching up to us, the last few minutes especially.

Upon arriving at the airport, the cameras and reporters had largely disappeared. It was hard to believe it had been fewer than twenty-four hours since the mob scene that greeted our arrival. We easily went to the gate and boarded the plane. I have very little recall of the hour-and-a-half flight back to Washington. I think I might have been a little numb.

When we landed at Reagan National Airport, it was clear things had changed. Waiting for me on the tarmac were two marked capitol police cars and one of their large black Suburbans. We piled into the Suburban and headed for home. I was concerned about how Liz and my kids might be reacting to the death threats and security issues, but Susan assured me that they had been contacted and were handling it well.

A security detail such as this leaves almost nothing to

chance. But they hadn't counted on a temperamental garage door opener I should have fixed or replaced a long time ago. As we drove around the back alley of my house, I saw a number of capitol police officers at my garage. One of them had the door opener, and when he saw us, he pushed the button. As a number of his colleagues and we looked on, nothing happened. I had gotten out of the Suburban but knew immediately, from prior experience, no amount of pushing the button was going to open the door.

We got back in the Suburban and went around to the front of the house. The small motorcade drew attention, and as I got out of the car, many people walking along the street stopped and began clapping and calling to me. I was tired but was surely appreciative of this spontaneous show of support. I was looking forward to sitting down, having a cold beer, and relaxing. However, after giving me a big hug and asking how I was feeling, Liz said, "Put on your old clothes, we've got a lot of work to do. Your little dance with destiny this past month has put us way behind and company is coming tomorrow!"

And so I ended one of the most momentous days of my life—in old clothes, painting and cleaning the house.

HOME IS not where you live, but where they understand you.

CHRISTIAN MORGENSTERN

SIX

Afterword

Shrewsbury, Vermont

July 4, 2001

Having consistently underestimated the reaction to my decision in the midst of it, I continue to be amazed at the response more than a month later.

Today, down in Warren, Vermont, the little town's Independence Day parade is featuring what's billed as a massive float celebrating my decision entitled "Happy Independents' Day," complete with the Capitol dome and my likeness bursting jack-in-the-box style through the top. The other night as I walked home from the Capitol down Pennsylvania Avenue, people eating at the sidewalk restaurants broke out in applause. And tomorrow I head back to Burlington to mark the release of the Magic Hat Brewery's latest offering, Jeezum Jim Ale.

This will soon pass. The American people will move on, and so will I. But it has opened my eyes to several things. First, it's often the reaction that is more telling than the action. Second, people must inevitably look at events through their own prisms. And finally, there seems to be a hunger in our country for heroes, especially of the political variety.

These are far-from-novel concepts. As Shakespeare wrote in *Hamlet* four hundred years ago, "The play's the thing, wherein I'll catch the conscience of the King." And in this play, personalities have been on vivid display.

The weekend before my announcement, Trent Lott described our relationship by saying, "We are friends, and have been for a long time." On conservative radio talk shows eight days later, he bitterly denounced my decision as "a coup of one." Aside from the rather regal implications, his statement showed the direction in which Lott inevitably turns, toward partisan battle in which Democrats are the enemy rather than the loyal opposition. A week later, he drafted a memo calling for a "war on the Democrats." In the context of the death threats coming in, some of Trent's more bellicose comments were particularly unwelcome. His political instincts, I am afraid, easily trumped whatever friendship we had, at least for now.

Such outbursts might simply be written off to the heat of the moment or an attempt to shore up his political standing with conservatives. But they are part of a pattern. At one point early in my chairmanship of the

Health and Education Committee, Lott handed me a small photo of Senator Kennedy on which he had used a felt pen to draw a red circle with a diagonal slash through it, the international sign for prohibition. It was meant as both a joke and a message: don't cooperate with Democrats, especially Ted Kennedy.

The President's top political adviser, Karl Rove, along with some of his colleagues, responded to my decision by trying to smear me, suggesting that my motivation was for a better committee assignment or some such nonsense. I'm sure part of his motivation was to deflect blame from the White House, but I suspect, too, that he may have believed it. For a purely political creature such as he, there had to be more to my story. What's conscience got to do with it?

For the better part of two weeks, the White House and Senator Lott were engaged in a not-so-subtle effort to deflect blame for my decision. The press was trying to track down every possible motivation for it. "Who Lost Jim Jeffords?" was the common refrain. Was it because I was snubbed by the White House during the National Teacher of the Year ceremony? Was I angered at Trent Lott for his trying to micromanage the education bill?

There were more theories than truth. The fact is that everyone made mistakes, myself included. But the fissure was really caused not by one or two events but by much slower moving political plate tectonics. The national Republican Party has shifted to the South and West, leaving Vermont and the Northeast behind, achieving through the ballot box what the Georgia Senate failed to secure with Irish backs. Just as Vermont quickly abandoned the Whigs in the 1850s, so do I think it will gradually leave the Republican Party of today if this party continues in the same direction.

The two political parties are undergoing an ideological purification, which I regret having contributed to. It has been under way for decades, at least since the Johnson Administration in the 1960s. The ranks of moderate Republicans have shrunk bit by bit, almost to a last redoubt in New England. Through retirement and death, the Senate has lost fine Senators like Bill Cohen, Jack Danforth, Mark Hatfield, Nancy Kassebaum, Warren Rudman, and John Chafee. While John has fortunately been replaced by his son Lincoln, who shares his political philosophy, his death in the fall of 1999 was nevertheless a deep loss for me personally, and for the Republican Party politically. His was a quiet voice of reason. With his passing, the voice of the moderates became quieter still. Were he still alive, I'm not sure my course would have been the same.

The Republican Party wants to define itself by cutting taxes, and if it can accomplish anything else, so much the better. This can be a winning political message, and I certainly don't begrudge my colleagues for adopting it. But I continue to believe in a more active role for the federal government. The late Mavis Doyle, the former dean of the Vermont press corps, often remarked that the duty of a journalist was to "comfort the afflicted and afflict the comfortable." I might soften it a bit, but I don't think that is too far from the proper role for government. My former Republican colleagues and I might have papered over these differences for a while, but sooner or later I think they would have yielded the same result.

Many of my colleagues have followed their better angels. I have been touched by those who have been able to overcome their anger. Former Singing Senator and now Attorney General John Ashcroft has been extremely decent. I'm sure he disagreed with me, but he made a point of calling me to assure me of our continued friendship. I suspect that the same deep-seated Christianity that gives liberals pause in his official capacity impels John to place some things above even the handing of power to liberals.

For most Americans, the response has been overwhelmingly positive. Expectant mothers called my office saying they planned to name their babies for me. The office was deluged with bouquets and good wishes. And my classmates at Yale interrupted our forty-fifth reunion to watch the speech and sign and send me a touching tribute.

Vermonters weighed in to my offices about ten to one in support of my decision. A month and a half later, the newspapers continue to receive letters to the editor praising and pillorying my switch. I thought it fair that Vermonters who had supported me financially in last fall's campaign should be provided refunds if they wished for them, not knowing how much money would be sought by erstwhile supporters. We haven't plowed through all the mail yet, but so far thousands upon thousands of people from Vermont and across the country have sent me contributions, while only a handful of Vermonters have asked for their money back. Lest this be the final verdict, at least one conservative organization has sent a mailing to my contributors decrying my decision, urging them to request a refund and giving them a preprinted, postage-paid request form to do so. So far, it has cost them far more than it has cost me. But I suspect the real purpose, as it usually is with these mailings, was to generate revenues for the organization doing the soliciting.

I cannot describe how flattered I am by the genuine response I have received, but I have to believe it is about a lot more than me. I think people are so frustrated by what they see of politics at the national level that they are famished for any indication that it is not so corrupt as they believe, that individuals will act on principle. Once they see it, they seize upon and invest in it maybe even more than it deserves.

Some people saw my decision as vindication of a presidential election they felt had been stolen. That certainly was not my aim, although I hope the President will govern more from the middle. I did what I thought was right. It will have some consequences. People I thought were friends were revealed as not to be; people who were indeed friends have grown distant. My place in the Senate has become an unfamiliar one, even more unfamiliar than being a moderate Republican in a conservative caucus. But time will mend much of today's discomfort. And the next election will sweep away the events of the past few months like a high tide erasing the afternoon's footsteps. But perhaps people will come to understand that there are a lot of Senators on both sides of the aisle like me—not famous, not perfect, but doing our best to serve our consciences and our constituents rather than our caucus. And if they don't believe that their representative meets this standard, perhaps they will work to find someone who does or run for office themselves.

I hope though, that my decision will prove to be a catalyst for change. The Senate adopted an amendment by Senators Hagel and Harkin to the pending education bill that will require full mandatory funding for special education over the next seven years. I hope the Senate conferees will hang tough and that we will be able to convince our counterparts in the House to accept it. There is a chance the response of some in the House could be to resist the Senate in part so that my decision will have a price. I hope that is far too cynical an approach for anyone to take, since the costs would be borne not by me but by disabled children. But it is not beyond the pale of political thinking in Washington.

Beyond this particular issue, I hope my decision will move the two parties to the center, where the American people are. The American people want an active, responsible federal government. The Republican Party was the party of Lincoln, but its claim to that mantle is uncertain today. As the nation fractured, Lincoln rededicated it to the principle that all men were created equal. He effected that principle not just through the Emancipation Proclamation and the Civil War, but by signing into law the Land Grant College Act of 1862. Liberty, and access to both land and higher education, would be the birthright of all Americans.

———

The Land Grant College Act was designed to provide the same opportunity to the sons of farmers and mechanics as had been available only to the scions of the upper class. It was the handiwork of Vermont Representative and later Senator Justin Smith Morrill, whose efforts had been stymied in the previous Congress by the veto of Democratic President James Buchanan. Morrill had been elected as a Whig in 1854, defeating a Republican in the process, but switched to the Republican Party before taking his seat in March of the following year. In addition to revolutionizing higher education in our nation, as chairman of the House Ways and Means Committee, he played a critical role in financing the Civil War that held it together.

In the nineteenth century, Republicans were the party of the progressives. And at the turn of the century, the Republican Party was in the forefront of what was then the environmental movement, with Vermonter George Perkins Marsh leading the way. Perkins was aghast at the deforestation of our hillsides and the destruction of our streams. There was an admixture of religion, a sense of stewardship, and plain common sense.

But the wellspring of the Republican Party was the cause of equal rights for all Americans, including those who came to this country in the bowels of slave ships.

The party was willing to sacrifice tremendous amounts of blood and treasure for this cause. Hardly a small town in Vermont lacks a memorial on the village green where scores of Civil War casualties are listed. At Gettysburg, Maine and Vermont again worked in tandem.

Much as we think the world has changed in the last hundred and fifty years, the issues that gave birth to the Republican Party are still among our most important challenges. Will we strengthen public education and the ladder of opportunity it provides? Or will we decide through our funding decisions that this is not a very high federal priority? Will we leave the land better than we found it for our descendants a hundred and fifty years hence? Or will we be blinded by the ensuing crises and leave it despoiled? Will we accord full rights to all Americans? Or will we continue to condone the denial of the protections of our laws to those who are gay?

It is clear what I hope for. That is the kind of Washington I hope to forge with what little influence is available to me. We have crying needs in our society that we must tackle rather than ignore. And we can never even begin if we are consumed by trying to take petty partisan advantage at every opportunity. The Americans people, I hope, will not stand for it.

ACKNOWLEDGMENTS

A Senator's career is built only with the support of family, voters, constituents, and staff. My thanks to all.

This book was written with the collaboration of Mark E. Powden.

ABOUT THE AUTHOR

JAMES M. JEFFORDS has been a U.S. Senator from Vermont since 1989. Currently serving his third term, he is chairman of the Environment and Public Works Committee. He lives with his wife Elizabeth in Shrewsbury, Vermont, and Washington, D.C.